PARTICIPATIVE
TRANSFORMATION

T0271685

Participative Transformation

Learning and Development in Practising Change

*Roger Klev and
Morten Levin*

Routledge
Taylor & Francis Group

LONDON AND NEW YORK

First published 2012 by Gower Publishing

Published 2016 by Routledge
2 Park Square, Milton Park, Abingdon, Oxfordshire OX14 4RN
711 Third Avenue, New York, NY 10017, USA

First issued in paperback 2016

Routledge is an imprint of the Taylor & Francis Group, an informa business

Gower Applied Business Research
Our programme provides leaders, practitioners, scholars and researchers with
thought provoking, cutting edge-books that combine conceptual insights,
interdisciplinary rigour and practical relevance in key areas of business and
management.

British Library Cataloguing in Publication Data
  Klev, Roger, 1962-
    Participative transformation: learning and development in
    practising change.
    1. Organizational change. 2. Management--Employee participation.
    I. Title II. Levin, Morten.
    658.4'06-dc23

Library of Congress Cataloging in Publication Data
Klev, Roger, 1962-
  Participative transformation : learning and development in practising
  change / by Roger Klev and Morten Levin.
    p. cm.
  Includes bibliographical references and index.
  ISBN 978-1-4094-2378-2 (hbk)
  1. Organizational change. 2. Organizational learning. 3.
  Management--Employee participation. 4. Organizational sociology. I. Levin,
  Morten. II. Title.
  HD58.8.K575 2012
  658.4'06--dc23

                                                                    2012007148

ISBN 13: 978-1-138-27279-8 (pbk)
ISBN 13: 978-1-4094-2378-2 (hbk)

Contents

List of Figures

Acknowledgement

Whilst this is a book that has, in the main, been written by the two authors, rather than being an edited volume, we are greatly indebted to Ann W. Martin, Mara Senese and Emil A. Røyrvik who have each contributed a chapter in the section on work forms. Their contributing chapters have been very important because they highlight how participative development can be practised. We are very thankful for their contributions.

Preface

This book was initially planned as a translation of our Norwegian book *"Change as Practice – Change Management through Learning and Development."* We had ideas of how to make the book readable for an international audience, but rather unexpectedly and unplanned the translation process became a rich and stimulating learning experience. Gradually this version took its own path intellectually as well as practically, and this English version is a very different book from the Norwegian edition. The bulk of the original arguments and positions are kept, while others are developed or changed. We managed to keep a playful mind and were able to question former chains of arguments. Sometimes this lead to an improved understanding, while in other instances the original turned out to be well-reasoned. It has been great fun to spend almost a year on this book.

Unintentionally we ended up choosing a style with an emphasis on clear short arguments, in fact a style that we learned from the philosophical practitioner Philip Herbst (an argument that cannot be formulated in simple words is not clearly understood).

We are grateful to our Norwegian publisher (Fagbokforlaget A/S) for letting us, free of charge (and of copyrights), use the Norwegian text in a translated version. A special thanks to Fagbokforlaget's editor Knut Ebeltoft who supported writing the Norwegian versions and made it possible to create this English version. We also would like to thank to Linn Haraldsvik who made the first rough translation of the original manuscript into English.

Last but not least, thanks to the students at the Norwegian University of Science and Technology who have attended our course in Organization Development. Their critical and constructive engagement inspired us to write and rewrite this book.

Roger Klev and Morten Levin
Trondheim, Norway

About the Authors

Dr Roger Klev is Head of Leadership Development at Reinertsen AS and Associate Professor at Norwegian University of Science and Technology. He has over 25 years combined research and teaching at with very direct involvement in organizational and strategic change in a variety of companies. After obtaining his PhD he worked as an organizational researcher and as Research Director at SINTEF, the largest independent research organization in Scandinavia. He is active in major research projects and is a published author and conference speaker.

Morten Levin is a Professor at the Department of Industrial Economics and Technology Management, The Faculty of Social Sciences and Technology Management at the Norwegian University of Science and Technology in Trondheim, Norway. He holds bachelor degree in mechanical engineering, a master degree in operations research and graduate degree in sociology. Throughout his professional life, he has worked as an action researcher with a particular focus on processes and structures of social change in the relationship between technology and organization. He has been research director at SINTEF, has held research, teaching and examiner posts at the Royal Norwegian Defense research Establishment, universities throughout Scandinavia and Great Britain and Cornell University in USA.He has performed in industrial contexts, in local communities, and in university teaching where he has developed and directed four sequential Ph.D. programs in action research. The last two have been on regional development (EDWOR program). He is author of a number of books and articles, including Introduction to Action Research: Social Research for Social Change.

Introduction: The Practice of Leading Change

Does the world need yet another book on organizational change? There are an overwhelming number of titles on organizational change that are available in bookstores or on the net. Why do we have ambitions to contribute yet another book to the already crowded bookshelves? From our perspective we see two main reasons.

The first is based on a critique of the field. While organizational change has gained a lot of attention in the last decades there is a very clear gap between the academic discourse on the one side, and on the other side advice from management books that seek to address the practitioner in a self-help style. The research-based literature is strong in terms of systematic analysis and structure while the management-oriented literature has a solid backing in conveying concrete experiences and success stories. The academic writing is weak in connecting to practice while management books lack systematic reflection.

The second reason for writing this book is to argue that participation is at the centre of practising organizational change. Organizational change is seen as actively shaped by people in processes where they influence premises, design possibilities and shape change through their active involvement. Simply put, organizational members who participate in successful change through what they actually do have to be involved in the change process. Change comes about because employees and managers actively participate in the concrete change activities in the organization.

The aim of this book is to build a research-supported foundation for practising organizational change. One major problem limiting the pool of knowledge is that the research-based literature is still fragmented and often contradictory, as methods and theories are spread out in a diffuse landscape. Our strategy to come to grips with these inherent difficulties is to construct what we judge as a coherent theoretical foundation for the practice of leading organizational change.

The lack of integration between the theoretical work on organizing and change and the practice of leading change is a major concern. The dominant approaches of the "practitioner-oriented" management literature also fail to fill this gap because of conceptual and analytic weaknesses. We do not automatically rule out the insights gained in the more popular management literature on change management, but the applicability of these insights is judged based on how they contribute to the on-going professional discourse and not as stand-alone success stories or recipes. The aim of our contribution is to provide a theoretical model of organizational change and at the same time practical guidance to assist the practitioner in leading change. What, then, characterizes the essentials of organizational change?

First, effective organizational change will impact everyday work in broader strata in the organization, and employees and managers who are influenced should take part in change activities, just as every citizen in a democratic society should be involved at some level in deciding on developing the future of their society. Second, organizational change will be about people and understood accordingly as a social and psychological developmental process that obtains its momentum from active participation. The realization of the organization's goals depends on active engagement. Third, participation in change processes should be seen as a way to facilitate knowledge processes where social resources are mobilized to create change. Participation will at the same time builds local assets and internal capacity for change. Participation is essential in mobilizing knowledge for the better solutions as well as to build knowledge for future change processes. We will present these arguments in more detail in Chapter 5.

Before shifting focus to the participative model, it is necessary to substantiate the initial critique of the existing literature in the field. The essential problem is that the mainstream management literature is too simplistic and decoupled of theoretical discourses, and thereby loses some of its potential to guide smart and sound developmental processes. A range of ideas and perspectives are launched in this literature and they barely relate to other relevant publications in the field. Mundane perspectives are given as much space as well-founded positions. However, this literature fills the bookshelves and while we are obviously critical, we of course acknowledge its popularity and why it is important to understand the needs it seems to meet. For a more elaborate and elegant discussion of these issues, we refer the reader to Pfeffer and Sutton's (2006) book *Hard Facts, Dangerous Half-Truths and Total Nonsense*.

The mainstream management literature delivers its answers in different ways. Some present simple rules or methods, like the book *The One Minute Manager* (Blanchard and Johnson

1983). This book has sold more than 13 million copies, presumably to leaders who want to have better structure and more impact in their everyday practice. Others deliver answers through unveiling the "secrets" behind leaders who are already accepted as world class successes, like Jack Welch's *Jack: Straight from the Gut* (Welch and Byrne 2001). This book builds a rather self-glorifying personal account of the author's thoughts and leadership style, as he was one of the most well-known industrial leaders in his time.

The literature in leadership is complex, contradictory and ambivalent in terms of creating clear theoretical positions and practical recommendations. To be a leader is to face new challenges all the time. There are parallel initiatives, unforeseen problems and opportunities, different interests to relate to and high expectations from others both internally and externally. At the same time it is impossible to have the total overview and control. The combination of complexity, responsibility and lack of control make most leaders uncertain and in search of assistance and guidance to create a safe haven. In his book *Riding the Wave of Change* (1988), Gareth Morgan develops a metaphor envisioning management as balancing a surfboard on a breaking wave. The rider has to both understand the present dynamic forces and predict how the wave will change on the way to the shore. To master surfing it is necessary to practice both standing on the surfboard, and to be able to stake out and follow a course that makes it possible to ride the shifting wave. From an organizational perspective the implication is that a manager has to master promptly today's tasks and at the same time make preparations for meeting future strategic challenges. This foresightedness lies in being able to see both where challenges may arise (see the fracture lines), and at the same time have the capacity to handle the foreseeable needs for adaptation. This capacity and ability to adapt is the essence of leading change. Proficiency in change and development is not a trait that appears automatically. It has to be deliberately developed to become an essential feature of the organization's daily operation.

Other contributions "explore" evidence of success at company level. In fact, one of these books may very well get the honour of being portrayed as the pioneer of making management literature global bestsellers. Peters and Waterman's runaway success *In Search of Excellence* (1982) was at the outset highly acclaimed, but was later criticized based on the evidence on which the conclusions were drawn. When Tom Peters "confesses" in a popular note how the book was created, it is an amusing and yet distressing story about the process of writing the book. In an internal project in McKinsey Corp his colleague Ben Waterman and himself were given the assignment to comment on the business aspects that high profile strategy thinking did not emphasize. The missing perspective was the organization of work, leadership and human resource. The authors were given enough funds to go where they wanted and talk to whoever they required, in order to investigate the actual phenomenon. They met with executives in top management positions and researchers and they were left with a lot of impressions, experiences and views of what shaped success. However, in preparing for a presentation to the Pepsi-Cola Company, it became necessary to abstract something essential from their "data". It would not be enough to tell a lot of disconnected stories. Tom Peters recollects the process behind the "main analysis" in the following way:

> *So here's what happened: The time was drawing near*
> *for the Pepsi presentation to take place. One morning*
> *at about 6:00, I sat down at my desk overlooking the*

San Francisco Bay from the 48th floor of the Bank of America Tower, and I closed my eyes. Then I leaned forward, and I wrote down eight things on a pad of paper. Those eight things haven't changed since that moment. They were the eight basic principles of Search. (http://www.fastcompany.com/magazine/53/peters.html)

The book became a huge success and it was the first management book to compete with popular novels on the *New York Times* bestseller list. Twenty years later a similar book made almost a parallel success, when Jim Collins and colleagues wrote a study in which they hunted for explanations for the difference between good and truly great companies (Collins 2001). This time the research design was more systematic, but once again the book ends up presenting the results as if this was the first to address strategy, leadership and change. There is absolutely no reference to other empirical research, concepts, models or theories. Patterns in the data material are transformed to a few points that serve as a practical guide to make a company great; pick the right people, choose products you are passionate about, create discipline and be a humble but decisive leader. It is delivered with stories and examples that make it a very inspiring. John Kotter's (1996) work *Leading Change* follows much the same pattern. Interpretation of interesting empirical material is transformed into recipes or steps, without relating the findings to existing theory and avoiding being explicit on how the empirical material was analysed. These steps can be recognized as wise, but at the same time it will not actually help the leader in the midst of the turbulence of real change.

What all these very popular, interesting and well-written books have in common is that they base their legitimacy on accounts of success, and our main critique is that they only present the insights that are assumed to give a direct guidance to success for others. Would leaders who decide to behave like Jack Welch become better leaders, even if they are obviously someone else? Is Welch's portrait of himself correct? Are the success stories true or are they just glorious self-deceptions not representing any particular value for other leaders? If told that successful companies have humble leaders, will leaders who try to be more humble experience that their company is more successful? If successful companies are conservative in using new technology, can that insight directly guide decisions on exploiting new technology-based opportunities?

Our point is that the learning processes that support and develop the practice of leading change are not to copy recipes or methods, but to be able to create collective reflections around our own and others' experiences as a basis for choosing, developing and modifying practical solutions and work forms that give change processes content and direction. An important part of leadership is the ability to meet the challenges of the uncertainty of the future.

Leading change is mastering the development of capacity for strategic change as well as being able to initiate and lead processes of organizational development (OD) aimed at solving pertinent practical problems. Change management is accordingly tied both to the development of preparedness for change, and having the capability to lead the practical processes necessary for the organization to develop and adapt to evolving practical challenges. Further on we will also argue that both developing preparedness and effecting strategies for change are based on broad employee participation.

Bridging the Gap Between Theory and Practice

The non-academic attitude in popular mainstream management literature also mirrors the obvious problem that much of the research-based knowledge of the field has little or no practical relevance. Definitions, theories and methodological approach in most of the research in the field on leadership are most unlikely to contribute to creating practical and useful solutions for the foreseeable future. There is, in other words, a fascinating situation where the pursuit of practical solutions is disconnected from the research-based knowledge, while knowledge developed through scientific procedures does not reach beyond the ivory tower of academia. Our ambition is to create theories that have practical relevance and build reflection and learning processes from local experiences.

Kurt Lewin's (1952: 169) statement "There is nothing more practical than a good theory" is without doubt an important guideline for the perspective in this book. We intend to shape an understanding of change processes built on research-based knowledge. At the same time it is our intention to create an understanding which is useful in practice. Our approach to the challenge of practically applicable knowledge development is based on research that is grounded in the scientific tradition of action research (Greenwood and Levin 2007, Reason and Bradbury 2007).

The leadership challenge in OD is to initiate and support change processes that the leader and the participants jointly engage in and take responsibility for the transformational activity. The factors and arguments supporting this position are shown in the following figure:

Figure I.1   Position of change management within the management field

The point of departure is a punctuated outline of the field of management and OD. These broad perspectives are narrowed down to conceptualizing of leading developmental processes and how these processes can facilitate local innovation and development. The core idea of the book is to build a theory and advise a praxis of participative organizational change with a special focus on leadership and participants.

PART I
TRANSFORMATION OF ORGANIZATIONS

People are inclined to see organizations as stable and permanent. A common perception is that they have been around forever, or at least as long as memory stretches back in time. The public seem to prefer to see stability instead of transition, and this leads to a profound misunderstanding of stability as the normal and organizational transformation as the exception. The perspective of this book is to turn this argument up-side down. We see transformation and change as the stable process while stability is an unsteady state, and this is in clear opposition to the dominant perspective on organizational change inherited from Kurt Lewin's (1943) "iceberg" metaphor: This model has three phases; unfreeze – change – freeze (untie roles and structures – change them – create a new stable structure). As a contrast we see the transformational processes as a continuous flow of small or larger incremental and evolutionary changes. That is the grounding perspective developed in this book.

The point of departure is a short tour through the literature on organizational theory. The intention with Chapter 1 is to investigate how different strands of organizational thinking conceptualize change. In Scientific Management and in theories of bureaucracy, change is viewed as transforming structures leading to an understanding that change emerges from making a new organizational blueprint. Modern perspectives build a dynamic perspective that organizations (and change) are shaped by the members' active involvement and accordingly that all organizational change is mediated by employee participation. No change will occur unless employees participate.

In Chapter 2 the focus is on how OD is constituted as a separate professional field. Different modes of practice and conceptualizations are discussed and the argumentation in the chapter points to participation as a central value and key driving force for change. The essential challenge in OD is to create a space for active participation and involvement by the people affected by the change. This is the important argument for the co-generative model of organizational change.

Before embarking on the co-generative model, it is necessary to step back and question the context within which organizational change take place (Chapter 3). Is it so that an OD process has no restrictions? This is of course a misleading perspective. All organizational change processes are constrained by the available technology because the organization of work is highly impacted by production technology. The socio-technical perspective informs this relationship. In addition, social and cultural norms and values will impact the transformation process. The national work culture and work life institutions (public institutions, trade unions, confederation of employers etc.) will create possibilities and shape constraints for what change processes can be effective. In short, all organizational change processes are constrained or made possible by technology and the political economy (culture, history, traditions and economic institutions).

In Chapter 4 the co-generative model is introduced as the central conceptualization of organizational change. This is a participative model where a change agent or a change leader join with the participants (problem owners) in an experimenting and learning activity in order to construct new organizational solutions. The change process emerges through the creation of new organizational structures, practices and individual skills and the subsequent evaluation and learning whether the actions had the desired outcome. The change moves forward in circles of experimentation, reflection, learning and subsequently new actions. In this learning process the focus will shift as new knowledge and understanding is created.

In Chapter 5, learning and knowledge are in focus. Different modes of learning are discussed and alternative forms of knowledge are presented. In a change model that builds on learning and knowledge creation, it is important to see the spectrum of knowledge from tacit knowing to explicit knowledge and in addition to understand the relationship between cognitive and organizational learning.

Chapter 6 pays attention to participation in change processes. Different forms of participation are addressed and special attention is given to resistance to change. Basically resistance to change emanates as rational reactions to change processes where control over the development is either unclear or still in the hands of leaders who are not participating in the change process.

Finally, in Chapter 7 the threads are pulled together in modelling leadership in change processes and in resource generation processes as a co-generative developmental process. The essential issue is to see leadership as a process of creating learning opportunities that will develop the employees' capacity both to handle daily work and to enable active involvement in long term strategic change.

1 Organizational Theory and Organizational Change

What is an organization?
How does the organization become what it is?
How is the organization changed?

There are different schools of thought when it comes to answering this overall question: "What is an organization?" One possible answer might be "an organization is a division of work which is coordinated and controlled by management, and that produces a planned outcome". Based on this thinking, change is about design and redesign of the organization and a top down approach to change is almost mandatory. Another possible answer is: "the organization is what its members create by their everyday practices". In such a perspective change is very much about how people inside the organization transform the way they think and act, inviting a more bottom-up and participative approach.

There have been many attempts to present a formal definition of an organization or to deal with the concept of organization. The authoritative work of March and Simon (1958) entitled *Organizations* omits for example any definition of an organization. Bolman and Deal (1984) present organizations as complex, surprising, deceptive and ambiguous, which could describe almost any kind of social institution. In fact, it does not clarify very much. Another major book in the field is Morgan's (1986) *Images of Organization* where the author bypasses the whole issue of definition by stating that an organization is best understood through associations with a wide set of metaphors. A fascinating approach to organizations is also presented by Hatch and Cunliffe (2006) where the authors detour the definition by presenting organization "theory" as a way of mapping a certain kind of activity as something called an organization. What social life in an organization is, depends on the theory (conceptual construction) that is applied, whether it is a metaphor or a conceptual frame.

These three questions in the introduction could serve as an introduction to a lengthy philosophical and substantive debate, but that is not our intention. Instead, we see the questions very much as practically grounded. Anyone who takes on the challenge of making significant changes in an organization will indeed have to ask themselves the pragmatic questions: "why is the organization the way it is, and how could it become different?" and "why should this particular approach make anything happen?" This creates the backdrop for how our thinking about participative transformation relates to these underlying assumptions about what makes an organization.

Organizations as Stable Structures: Classical Organization Theory and Top-Down Change

By the beginning of the twentieth century, certain ideas about organization theory already had a lasting impact on the substantive theoretical issues in the field and on how human work is conceptualized. This is often referred to as the classical structural thinking in organization theory, and the main features were bureaucratic institutions, hierarchical power, clear organizational communication lines, division of labour and specialization. Two people are associated with these conceptual developments. The German sociologist Max Weber (1978/1922) presented an understanding of the bureaucratic structure of public administration where the core issue was to support a public service that was impartial, efficient and stable. On the other side of the Atlantic, the US-based engineer Frederick Taylor (1911) coined and formalized what he saw emerging in manufacturing as scientific management Fragmentation of work (separating manual and intellectual labour) combined with control systems would create an economically efficient production system.

Classical organization theory was formed during and as a consequence of a social and technological period of massive industrialization. The industrial structure of the Western countries in the mid-nineteenth century consisted mainly of relatively small craft-based manufacturing companies. By the end of the century, the Industrial Revolution led to the rise of significantly larger manufacturing companies. The interaction of new technologies, mass production, capitalism and strong monopolies created a growing working class and a new industrial reality. At the same time, research became substantially more important, not just within science and technology, but in the emergence of new professions (anthropology, psychology and sociology), which made human beings and social interactions objects of science. Mass production created entirely different challenges and possibilities that, alongside the development of nation states in need of rational government, shaped the foundations of what we now know as classical organization theory.

Frederick Taylor personified the "mechanical" organization of human work. In his short and prosaic book *Principles of Scientific Management* (1911), Taylor argues for the potential inherent in the scientific design of work. This latency, if applied in a proper manner, would improve a company's efficiency and profit as well as workers' wages and health. In Taylor's "Scientific Management", tasks were to be performed according to predetermined criteria and rules. Taylor described a system where the first step was to study every detail of the individual jobs. Every single operation was scrutinized, so that the most efficient performance could be defined. Based on this analysis, the idea was to select the worker with the correct set of capabilities to do the job, train them, pay them by piece rates and keep them under close supervision by the shop floor foreman. Particularly in combination with assembly line technology and mass production (also known as Fordism, named after Henry Ford), this approach was highly profitable. A characteristic feature of this production system is the separation between processes of tight management planning and control and the subsequent manual execution. This process can be seen as the first significant step towards specialization both on the shop floor and of management functions. Today a final stage in the Tayloristic mode is approached when company functions are outsourced (that is, moved from the manufacturing organization to other specialized units or firms). The result of the Tayloristic approach was manufacturing organizations where people were viewed as disposable cogwheels in a complete and detailed production machinery.

Another main pillar of classical organization theory is the bureaucracy model. For many practitioners, "bureaucratic" is synonymous with inefficiency and almost unchangeable organizational structures. There is hardly any organizational phenomena that are more contradictory in people's minds than "change" and "bureaucratic". The rational foundation of bureaucracy is to ensure that everyone receives equal treatment based on the objective content of needs and factual problems. Each case is to be solved based on rules and not by personal whim. Bureaucracy is basically meant to be an ultimate impartial and rational system of administrative procedures and decision-making. The career pattern is quite predetermined. The route is the move up to the next level in order to gain more authority, control and power. The positions are impersonalized in the sense that an employee in any position can be changed without impacting the factual operation of the organization.

Bureaucracy is highly critiqued and two lines of critical assessment are dominating. First, a bureaucratic organization is difficult to change and the transformation process has to come from higher echelons in the organization. Second, bureaucracy might be dysfunctional because it creates vicious circles of inefficiency (Crozier 1964).

In the Tayloristic and Weberian thinking, an efficient organization is a unit characterized by rational decision-making processes (where personal preferences and whims have no place). The organization has a well-defined hierarchical authority (everyone knows who is their boss), and which has a clear-cut division of work and specialization with a distinction between planning, decision-making and actual performance of work. This is perhaps the most important link between classical organization theories and approaches to change that we find as dominant today; the clear separation in time and roles between planning, decision-making and concrete practice. This basic understanding will of course invite a top-down or expert-driven approach to organizational change. Change is seen as a consequence of rational analysis that subsequently leads to redesign which initiates a separate process of implementing the decided changes.

The Ultimate Expert Driven Redesign: Business Process Reengineering (BPR)

The most elaborate example of this thinking was the global wave of Business Process Reengineering in the mid-1990s. When it comes to powerful marketing of a new management fad, few can rival Business Process Reenginering (BPR) (Hammer 1990; Hammer and Champy 1993). The main thesis in BPR is the exploitation of the opportunities provided by IT to carry out work processes (particularly those related to so-called business processes) in a completely different way. In many cases, early information and communication technology (ICT) based solutions were applied to automate old and often cumbersome work processes. Instead the BPR ethos was to see ICT-solutions as an opportunity to take giant leaps and to think and act in completely new ways, using the end-product as a starting point for the systemic analysis. The most controversial aspect of BPR was the message to completely disregard old ways of working. Building on experience, its proponents said, was the same as paving cattle trails when a new motorway was the best solution.

The "Clean sweep!" recipe required making a fresh start where experts could work out the best solutions. Even though the main message was to prepare the company for the ICT age, time was turned back to Frederick Taylor. The "one best way" and the expert-based methods of designing other people's workday were reintroduced with great force. This is precisely the ethos of Scientific Management. The popularity of BPR led to impressive financial resources being allocated to the change efforts, but as companies embarked on BPR processes considerable critique was launched. Worldwide evaluations of BPR projects concluded with rather disappointing results, in particular compared to the ambitions and promises. According to Thomas Davenport, referring to a 1994 survey of BPR projects "67% were judged as producing mediocre, marginal, or failed results" (Davenport 1995). The supporters and true believers of BPR often explained this as a consequence of projects not being sufficiently radical or carried through with enough force. For others, including Thomas Davenport, one of the trend's early supporters, the reflection in hindsight was that BPR was "the fad that forgot people" (Davenport 1995). Adaptation and change were understood as purely technical processes, and not as human development and adaptation.

Responding to the Japanese: Manufacturing and Improvement Concepts

Although BPR was extreme in its approach, it was far from alone in a market that promises to deliver clear recipes for good organizing and change processes. From the 1980s there was a growing recognition in Western industries that Japanese manufacturing companies, particularly in the car industry, had an advantage because they could manufacture and deliver products more reliable and cheaper than foreign competitors. How could this be? A first answer was that the Japanese had a different way of thinking about production and quality. This distinctive approach was named "Total Quality Management" (TQM), and was communicated as something far more than techniques, because quality was founded on philosophy, attitudes, organizational design and leadership and communication. Instead of correcting errors in the final product control, the idea was to build quality into every single

21

step in the production process. The effect of TQM was to avoid errors in the first place by improving the organization, administrative systems and employees' attitudes. In the wake of TQM, a number of new concepts and practices for efficient production were introduced as new perspectives explaining why Japanese manufacturing companies were so competitive. Examples were production control, supply chain management, quality and logistics. "Just in time" and "lean production" were phrases that emerged as a way to coin the Japanese mode of production. The idea behind "just in time" production was to enable increased security of delivery and reduce in-process inventory. "Lean production" focussed on eliminating superfluous inventory and unnecessary work, but also on getting rid of machines and tools that were not needed.

Management Fads

New concepts, solutions, and recipes are emerging at a seemingly constant rate. These new trends or fads can be interpreted as a response to a new understanding of basic challenges and opportunities in business life. Fads like Balanced Scorecard (Kaplan and Norton 1996) argue for a focus on enablers (factors that produces results) instead of on the results themselves. If improvement has to take place, the effort must be to change the enablers. Other examples include Intellectual Capital (Edvinsson and Malone 1997) which seeks to measure intangible values, and Corporate Social Responsibility which gives guidance to companies which will operate ethically and legally in a very complex global arena. We will not relate to the substance and promises of such new trends in business management, but just point to the fact that there is a huge market for concepts that promise certain results if the company implements the new solution. Most of these have very predesigned solutions developed by experts, and the challenge in change process is typically defined as a process of implementation. It is fair to say that most companies experience such processes of implementation as more challenging that they have hoped and/or expected.

These trends or fads seem to have a fairly short lifetime. Every three to five years a new "promising" trend or fashion is introduced and they are usually connected to management "gurus". Micklethwait and Wooldridge presented a critical analysis of these fads in their book *The Witch Doctors* (1996). They point to the close relationship between gurus and international consulting, where the fads create new market possibilities for consultancy. Another critical analysis is done by Bradley and colleagues (Bradley et al. 2000); in their perspective, fads become the myths that are the safety harness for hard proven businesses.

Scientific management and the theory of bureaucracy established the important principle of a clear division between intellectual activity in planning and control of production and the actual concrete practices. This principle paved the way for top-down and expert-driven approaches to change. Whilst BPR takes this to the extreme, our argument is that the separation between intellectual and manual work are more the rule than the exception in mainstream approaches to organizational change. In the last decades, however, other perspectives have emerged in organization theory and shaped quite a different set of relations between organizations, people, work and change.

Organizations as Practices and Change as Learning

From the early 1980s, new voices appeared in organization theory that saw organizational members less as parts of a machine and more as actively engaged in producing organizational reality. From an academic position, Chris Argyris and Donald Schön (1978) introduced perspectives such as practice, theories of action and organizational learning. In their view, an organization is not primarily explicitly designed, but is rather the product of what people do, how they interact and what they learn. A few years later Peters and Waterman (1982) wrote *In Search of Excellence* in which they claim, "the secret to success is not in structure and systems designed by managers and experts". Rather, corporate success depends on shared values and hands-on leaders who see and treat the employees as resources who can and will create excellence.

Later contributions followed the same line and tended to explain what the organization is and might become as a result of action and interaction between organizational members, rather than as a result of deliberate decisions and planning. Conceptualizing organizations who are able to learn and develop become crucial.

Organizations Can Learn

Chris Argyris and Donald Schön (1978, 1996) published their canonic work on organizational learning in 1978. This book also made a significant contribution to understanding work. They developed a theoretical model where employees base their practices on their own "theories of action" which are learned through processes of reasoning and reflection integrated in concrete practice.. The essence is that everyday organizational practice is learned, and that change in the organization must be understood as learning processes.

Argyris and Schön (1978, 1996) delivered convincing arguments that thoroughly erased the separation of thought and action. Whilst classical organization theory suggests that the natural starting point for change is management, Argyris and Schön (1996) hold that the separation of thought and action is not only unproductive but downright meaningless. Individual and collective reasoning will always form the basis for action. A theory of action perspective must have as a point of departure that new practices emerge from learning.

The concept "theory of action" is important for understanding what an organization is and how it can be meaningful to talk about learning processes at the organizational level. When the concept was introduced, just the idea that organizations are a collective that could "learn" was considered "perverted" thinking. Learning was previously seen solely as an individual cognitive and practical capacity. Action theories in the form of basic assumptions and established action strategies define and explain the activity in an organization. This is not to be understood as a plain sum of independent individual processes but as a mutually and collectively produced and held assumption of how to act. In other words, action theories at individual and organizational levels are a way of describing the organization as it is shaped and changed by learning processes over time.

From early 1990s there was a shift from discussing the phenomena of learning to a normative debate on how organizations might be developed such that they have an inherent capacity to learn. Arie de Geus (1997) introduced the concept of "learning organizations". The author described

25

how planning as an activity in Royal Dutch Shell changed from a detached analytic activity to becoming a well-structured learning process. The core idea was to utilize experiences from current activities as well as scenarios of possible activities to induce collective learning and an improved repertoire of actions. Ever more pronounced is Peter Senge's book *The Fifth Discipline* (1990) where he emphasizes in particular system thinking and system dynamics as a core approach to accomplish a learning organization. The "fifth discipline" was the systemic thinking that the author held as a vital factor in everyday operational life. Through understanding the contextual factors and the interrelationship between activities in the organization, the learning capabilities can be enhanced.

This new school viewed organizations primarily as arenas for knowledge creation. The essential factor for sustainability was the ability to be smart in developing and utilizing knowledge. It was important to understand what constitutes knowledge and learning, and which organizational mechanisms and personal skills controlled knowledge development in organizations. This was obviously a radically different point of departure from what was found in traditional organization theory. This perspective was concerned with capabilities and qualifications, rather than concrete and tangible structures and practices. Survival and success were not ensured through structural solutions but through building the organization's capacity and ability to utilize the technological and human resources to continuously create necessary solutions and realize opportunities. The discourses on "learning organizations" were concerned with understanding conditions for learning as fundamental elements of organization and management, rather than as sudden responses to potential crisis. The perspective that organizations have the ability to learn is a prerequisite for arguing that organizations continuously change. Organizations are in a continuous state of change which is also the force that promotes learning for new actions to be taken in the organization. The essential question is what makes an organization operate effectively in a learning modus? The learning organization school provides some answers, but there is little proof that the insights about what make organizations learn has developed a foothold in business life. For example, Argyris and Schön (1996) strongly argue for the need of developing a Model II thinking (see Chapter 5) in organizations, and at the same time comment that there are few examples of organizations that manage to live up such a model. Even textbooks in OD use Lewin's (1943) structural theory (unfreezing – change – freezing) as a core concept for change, rather than developing approaches and models based on change as learning. There are, however, important and interesting exceptions in the recent turn in organization theory. Theorists seem to be ready to be more interested in what people in organizations do and how their sense-making produces organizational realities such as structure, communication lines and control procedures.

Organizations and Change as Product of its Members

One of the most elaborate and influential theoretical contributions to how people produce the organizational reality they operate within is formulated by Karl Weick (1995), who made an important step towards describing organizations as dynamic systems. His initial position was that sensemaking in organizations takes place when members develop an understanding (sense) of the job they perform through their actual work. This sensemaking occurs in the interaction between concrete performance of work and the interpretation of what the work means. Weick describes the process this way; "The concept of sensemaking highlights the action, activity, and creating that lays down traces that are interpreted and then reinterpreted" (Weick 1995: 13). The point is that understanding what it means to work in an organization is developed through interpretation of the daily work. The idea was that an organizational solution (structure) in the form that can be drawn on a piece of paper is just a point of departure for how the organization actually would operate. The concrete and functional organization is developed through performing work emerging from the suggested organizational solution. There will of course be pressure to work in new ways, but the functional and working organization is only established when people make sense of the new work form. This sensemaking is a collective process whereby people jointly develop a retrospective interpretation. Through solving day-to-day tasks, an understanding of what it means to work in the specific organization will gradually be developed. Members of the organization will be able to choose between two strategies to solve concrete tasks. First they can *exploit* what they already know and understand; or second, they can *explore* new creative solutions (March 1991). Weick's sensemaking perspective is important because it indisputably places the human being at the centre of the process of creating a new organization. It is through developing a new, concrete way of performing work that each person understands and interprets the job.

This is an essential argument for the participation of employees in the actual design of an organization. Management can dream up blueprints for the ideal organization, but it will never see the light of day if people do not act in accordance with the printed expectations. Through the employee's concrete actions the new organization emerges. No new organization can work without the individual employee being involved in making sense of and developing the necessary skills to do the job. Great external pressure and significant use of force can be applied, but in the end individual employees need to figure it out for themselves. In an organizational change perspective, Weick's (1995) sensemaking is important because it actually depicts dynamic knowledge processes. Understanding what it means to work in an organization is developed precisely through reasoning about the performance of work, which then describes a dynamic and continuous process.

In the perspective given above, an organization is not seen as produced by a management blueprint, but is produced and reproduced in processes of learning and sensemaking in daily work. This frames the essence of organizational change as a process engraved in the employees' daily work. Organizational change emerges from what they do, how they reflect upon what they do, how they interact and communicate and how their understanding may then be changed to become a basis for changing practices. Whilst the classic structural organization theories invite top down change approaches, the understanding of organizations as produced by their members in everyday work and interaction clearly advocates a participatory perspective of change. In this perspective, change is not by design but by process.

2 Change as Praxis – Organizational Development as a Professional Field

The fundamental perspective of this book is based on theories of social change. These insights provide an understanding of change as a social phenomenon and support guidelines for how development processes should be designed and facilitated. The role of research-based knowledge is also to enable a more shared understanding of challenges and possibilities between participants. That is, research-based knowledge does not provide ready-made solutions, but is a resource for the participants in their efforts to change. Thus, research-based knowledge should ideally communicate well to all participants and the facilitator should act as a skilful translator in order to make such knowledge accessible for all participants in the change process.

The main knowledge base is theories and models formulated within the organizational development (OD) tradition. It is an important message in mainstream OD that developmental work should be grounded in the organizational members' work situation. However, the OD tradition mainly pertains to internal organizational problems like conflicts, communication, cooperation and training. Likewise, the OD practitioner involved in organizational change typically focuses on processes and does not engage in substantial discussions about specific solutions in the organizational change processes. Our position, as a contrast, conceptualizes the leader or the change agent as an active participant not only in designing development processes but also in shaping understanding of problems and solutions. This constitutes a significant distinction from mainstream OD, and will be discussed in depth in Chapter 3. Another distinction is that most OD approaches emphasize how processes can be designed to address particular problems, while we emphasize developing the organization's capacity and ability to change through working with real and important problem-solving processes. Thus the perspective on leading organizational change management is to *master the development of capacity for change and also to be able to initiate and lead processes of development.*

Further, it is obvious that the practice of organizational change should be based on values. Realized change does not have the same significance independent of how it is achieved. We value work life democracy and it is most unlikely that a democratic institution can be created by undemocratic means. Work is an important ingredient of people's lives, and working with organizational change is thus not to design and redesign some kind of machinery but to influence the present and future development of people. For the practitioner, there is no escape from participating in processes where there are a variety of interests, goals and development trajectories, and they would have to judge what to maintain and support. This should also be reflected in theories of organizational change. Participation is a value-based position and is essential in creating a sustainable model for deliberate change and the transformational processes should reflect this important foundation.

The History and Influence of OD Approaches

A professional field does not emerge overnight. It is often the situation that some scattered activities or projects at different institutions work on parallel issues that in hindsight can be interpreted as systematic efforts that all point in the same direction. This is undoubtedly the situation in OD. What can eventually be identified as the field of organizational development emerged because researchers and professionals with backgrounds in various social sciences wanted to use the research-based knowledge to meet societal challenges. Social sciences were traditionally strictly empirical and thus retrospective. The early practitioners of what would now be defined as OD wanted to use social science insights proactively. In OD, professionals would have a varied background including such disciplines such as psychology, sociology, anthropology, pedagogy, engineering and economics. The practitioners' academic backgrounds vary greatly, but they seem to share a common perspective in using models of human activity as a basis to guide development activities. In addition, some champion democracy and participation, while others are more concerned with efficiency. It is in this landscape that some fragments of a map will be drawn, and hopefully make it possible to navigate the desired fairlead (route of change).

It is actually unclear when OD was coined as a distinctive concept. There probably existed parallel sources and "development groups" that established a foundation for the concept within social psychology. OD was presumably first used in the late 1950s by two American organizational theorists (Beckhard and McGregor) in a job they did at General Mills (French et al. 1994: 30). Eventually, OD became the term for a wide range of work forms in organizations that aimed for improvement, development, democratization, learning and increased efficiency.

A general feature of OD is that it is about planned change processes in organizations where a professional and external analysis is the basis for the change. The generic features of OD initiatives are that they are based on generating data about the work conditions in an organization, analysing the data and subsequently using it as a basis for initiating planned change.

As will be shown in the rest of this chapter, different practised OD approaches can be seen as variations of this generic model. The differences are primarily to be found in the relationship between the OD expert and the organization, and on how the learning processes were designed.

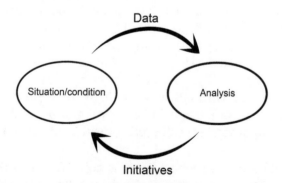

Figure 2.1   The generic structure of the OD process

T-groups (Training Groups)

In the late 1940s, change projects were initiated at MIT that had as a goal to develop leaders in the US. This institution later became the National Training Laboratory (NTL). Participants signed up for a form of training which was based on giving people feedback on how they cooperated and coexisted with other people. The process implied that a professional staff observed the participants in the training groups and analysed and reflected on how the participants related to each other. Based on these observations, the staff had a good foundation for deciding how best to help the groups' progress. So far, this is straightforward traditional handiwork for any professional using their skills to help others develop. What made this project particularly interesting from an academic point of view was that the group members wanted to be present when the staff had their more or less informal discussions about how the groups worked. The groups were allowed in, and the effects of this new work form were judged to be positive for the groups' and the members' learning. From being objects of experts' analysis, they then became participants in a shared process of reflection on and learning from their own experiences.

This could be seen as a story about pragmatic adjustments in the implementation of a development project. Quite the contrary; it is a big conceptual leap. This way of working in T-groups showed how important it was for the learning process to let people participate in reflection on their own activities. It is both a matter of understanding how learning occurs, and also what is and should be the roles and relationships between so-called experts and those who are "objects" of development work. T-group projects represented very early strategies for involving people in participative change processes. Participation by the problem owners is today not only an important part of OD, but is certainly a prerequisite for describing processes as OD.

Personal experiences
and staff observations

Group processes

Shared reflection

New understanding of one self
and the group

Figure 2.2   OD process – T-groups

Sensitivity training, as part of the T-group activity was often named, had a great impact specifically in training managers. Sensitivity training became a vehicle for improving the managers' understanding of themselves and their work that would hopefully enable them to run the business in a better way. In the 1970s and 1980s, there was a wave of programmes and courses aimed at helping managers to become new and better leaders. Some of the courses went very far in creating extreme situations for the participants and "breaking them down," then attending to re-building the participants to a new and presumably "better" self-understanding, and included attitudes and communication skills that would improve their leadership. The pedagogical profile of these modern training groups is grounded on an idea of growth through strength and confidence, rather than stress and uncertainty. Much of this sensitivity training was ethically questionable basically because the participants were not supported enough after having been psychologically dissected. These variations are probably still on the market, but development, including leadership development, is to a far greater extent characterized by approaches that focus more on organizations and groups than individuals.

T-groups took a position as an important remedy in leadership training, and consequently a backdrop or environment for individual development. Today, groups are still essential tools in most OD initiatives, primarily because they make an intermediary between the large unit, where it is difficult to establish dialogues, and the myriads of individual initiatives, which are often difficult to organize. Large units can be divided into smaller groups that make communication and common reflection possible. Thus knowledge about groups and group processes still constitutes a central focus for practising OD.

The leading professional behind the development of T-groups at MIT was Kurt Lewin. He escaped from the rise of Nazism in Germany and in the years before the Second World War he worked at different US universities and research institutions. Towards the end of the war he was affiliated to MIT. The work with T-groups at MIT involved several professionals who eventually became important within OD. Chris Argyris, Warren Bennis and Douglas McGregor were all trained as team leaders in connection with the NTL.

Action Research

Action research (AR) is dedicated to social change and development. The general idea is that research and practical problem solving are two pieces carved out of the same log. Research-based knowledge is needed for solving practical problems as concrete solutions are the basis for new scientific knowledge.

AR is one of the most influential contributions to an academic understanding of and justification for OD. AR was an "outsider" for a long time in the social science circles of academia; always in need of explaining and defending its position towards more established positivistic approaches to research and knowledge and behaviouristic approaches to learning. Mainstream social research views it as important to keep a distance and not to become involved in the field of research. Within this frame of reference, researchers should at any cost avoid impacting the field under study. The researchers should only relate to the field through communicating the knowledge they have acquired through their research after the research community has assessed and accepted its validity. In contrast to this, AR presupposes that the researchers engage actively with the research field. The main principle in AR is that it should contribute to create useful knowledge for local problem-solving and at the same time use the data and experiences from this praxis as input for research-based knowledge generation. A prerequisite for this to happen is that learning takes place with those who "own" the field and not primarily with the researcher. A central theme in AR is to develop participants' knowledge. In addition, AR rests on a belief that knowledge is created through change. Consequently, one does not simply establish knowledge first and then make changes, but through the change process one acquires knowledge about a system or an organization, which then becomes a foundation for new initiatives. AR is facilitating action-oriented learning processes for participants, which is precisely the aim of OD.

AR's somewhat controversial position has created a need, from an AR point of view, to focus on what knowledge (and thus research) is, how it is created and disseminated, what roles so-called experts can and should have and, not least, how all this is connected to a notion of change processes. This focus has contributed substantially to OD theory.

Strategies for OD based on AR can be traced back to two institutional environments. The first is linked to Kurt Lewin. He delivered both theoretical and practical contributions which are considered by many as the first building blocks of what eventually became AR (Lewin 1943). The second environment was the Tavistock Institute in London, where researchers like Eric Trist, Fred Emery and Philip Herbst made important contributions to the development of AR. In this environment we also find the source of another main contribution to OD, namely the sociotechnical approach to organizational design and change.

Figure 2.3   OD process – action and reflection

Sociotechnical Theory and Strategies for Change

The sociotechnical school found a foothold in work life research and was both inspired by human relations tradition thinking (Mayo 1933), and impacted by industrial democracy. Central in this development was the London-based Tavistock Institute of Human Relations, which, in the first years after the Second World War, conducted a sequence of studies in British industry aiming at supporting the reconstruction of manufacturing in the UK. Researchers at Tavistock linked up with Norwegian partners and cooperated in the 1960s on an industrial democracy project in Norway. The project was a collaboration between the Norwegian Confederation of Employers and the Trade Union Council and the action research group. This project was path-breaking and developed among other things the semi-autonomous work groups, a social invention that spread around the world as "team based work" (Emery and Thorsrud 1969). Tavistock researchers Fred Emery and Eric Trist pioneered the development of sociotechnical thinking.

The fundamental idea in sociotechnical thinking is that an organization consists of both technological and social systems, and that the interaction between technology and people has a decisive influence on the total operation of the organization. One of the main principles in sociotechnical theory is that one has *choices* both in terms of what kind of technology to use and how to organize work in conjunction with the production technology. There is no given solution that is automatically best. This is in strict opposition to Taylor's fundamental position based on his scientific method of finding "the one best way." Sociotechnical thinking warns specifically against first making decisions on technology, and subsequently including people as "parts of the machine" or the prolonged arm of production technology. Neither should organizational solutions be locked in advance and then forced onto a production system. Sociotechnical thinking breaks away from the almost in-built assumption that hierarchy is the only relevant and possible organizational structure and Herbst (1977) was an early pioneer for network-based work organizations. An essential concept in sociotechnical theory is "joint optimization," which means to simultaneously consider both technology and social systems in searching for the optimal way of organizing. Technology should be judged from a social perspective and work organization should be considered from a technological position and through these mutual perspectives a joint solution should be found. In sociotechnical thinking it is further important as a part of the solution to create good working conditions very much in line with the ideas of humanistic psychology and also to create participation and democracy (Rogers 1969; Maslow 1954).

Choice of organization and management was seen as a consequence of the actors' involvement in the change process. Participation by those who would be affected by change became the foundation for the development work. To increase the degree of democracy at work is in line with the core values of sociotechnical design.

Sociotechnical theory was primarily a theory of work design, but eventually the change process itself became central. This was a consequence of democratic values and models in the research group that developed the perspective. Employees' participation in the process of redesigning work places turned out to be an essential feature of the design work. In addition, it was a significant point that those who worked in the organizations had the best prerequisites for understanding the technological as well as social conditions.

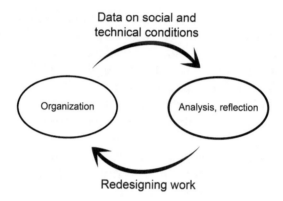

Figure 2.4   OD process – sociotechnical thinking

Survey Feedback

Survey feedback is a form of change-oriented praxis that came into use towards the end of the 1940s. The idea was the same as in the majority of all other OD work, namely to provide a social system (an organization) with a new and better self-understanding that could facilitate organizational improvement. The applied methodology was to have members of the organization to respond to a survey charting problems and possibilities in the local organization. The analysis of the data would subsequently lead to advice on the proper actions required in order to secure the health of the organization. This is fundamental thinking similar to making a diagnosis for an unhealthy organization.

The concrete practice of survey feedback started with asking all members of the organization to fill in a form prepared by the OD consultant. The factors and variables in this survey were often considered to be universal. The forms were then collected and run through a statistical analysis in order to identify particular problem areas. They were sometimes also run against other databases that could provide a basis of comparison with something regarded as "normal" or "best practice". In turn, the results were fed back to the organization, which could use them to recognize the prevalence of phenomena or problems, see problems one had not noticed, examine developments since earlier analyses and initiate concrete activity in order to repair the organizational problems.

The survey-feedback approach was considered OD because knowledge related to the life in an organization was referred back to the members of the organization. At the same time, it is significantly different from central parts of AR. Survey feedback is largely based on the assumption that "solid" data showed specific factors in the organization that needed improvement. An important point in AR (particularly since the 1980s) is that it often takes more than generalized data and "externally" created summaries to change people's theories and their behaviour. In AR, there is a much stronger focus on internal developmental processes of the organization than there is in approaches based on survey feedback.

Figure 2.5   OD process – questionnaires and reporting

Participation as a Fundamental Value and Practice

Professional activity will always be consciously or unconsciously rooted in ethical and value-based propositions. Questions of transparency, integrity, credibility, authenticity, authority and influence will label ethical and value-based frameworks for change. Our argument is that it is important to clarify the premises of the development effort. This provides greater transparency and predictability for all parties as to what can be expected in processes that will always have some inherent uncertainty.

Choices based on ethics and values have decisive influences on approaches to leading change. The literature in the field rarely clarifies which values and ethical premises are underpinning the change process. Such clarifications are important, and we base our reasoning on leading change on an ideal articulated as participatory democracy (Pateman 1970). The essence is a democratic right to exercise control over one's immediate and specific work and life conditions, and an honest participation in the change effort is a foundation of this perspective. In the broadest sense, leading change implies a systematic participative effort to develop and transform employees' work in order to reach strategic goals and to improve employees' control over their own situation. In a democratic society it is natural and important to extend the ideal of democracy to the workplace.

In a phase model of change (first plan, then train and finally implement), implementation is often regarded as the most time-consuming and expensive. The putting into practice phase is where the ready-made design is presented to the members of the organization, while the definition of problems and their solutions in that model have been taken care of by leaders and specialists. An important pragmatic argument for a more thorough participatory approach is that the expensive implementation process is less costly when employees themselves created the solution. Not only do they know the new practice but they also own the new way of working. In this perspective, the resources are used to think through challenges and options, make decisions that have broad support and find solutions that can be implemented with the employees. Resistance to change will arise at an early stage, not when costs have been incurred and implementation is the next step. Either the resistance can be determined and integrated in the development effort, or it can make it possible for those who do not want any participation in the development process to seek other positions.

OD as Co-generative Learning

OD, as it is portrayed in this book, rests heavily on participation and collective reflection. The co-generative learning model (see Chapter 4) is based on the argument that both participants and local leaders or change agents are engaged in the same learning and developmental process. The leaders and change agents bring both professional insight about social change and an understanding of how this can be facilitated in change and development processes. The change agents bring to the table in-depth knowledge about developmental processes while local leaders also convey in-depth experiences and understanding from their own organization. This knowledge is essential to the developmental process. Local knowledge is of course in the hands and the heads of the participants. In this way, continuous organizational change can take place when the actors are proactive in this effort. The challenge is to have the participants take on the responsibility for their own development.

Leading the Transformative Process: "The Change Master"

The field of organizational change has two distinct camps. One is construed from organizational development that has an expressed aim to utilize behavioural science as the conceptual platform for change processes. In addition, OD introduces the outside facilitator as a core actor in company-based change. The facilitator is responsible for planning the local activity and is a supporter of the whole transformative process. The other perspective of organizational change is change management. The conceptual foundation of change management is built almost exclusively on individual experiences and is seldom scrutinized in rigorous tests. It is practical, and the practitioners of change management often brag loudly of the achieved results. The perspectives in change management therefore dominate the change practices.

Our perspective is that organizational change should have ingredients from both camps. First, we have clearly argued for a value-base in participative processes. Pragmatically it is obvious that organizational transformation only occurs when people change, either they have a formal say in the transition or not. Second, participative change processes are the only way in which democratic organizations and a democratic society can be created.

Change processes do not come by themselves; they have to be led. This is a distinct type of leadership that aims at creating learning so that the individual members in the organization can grow and develop skills and competencies throughout the transformation activity. The leadership is markedly different from authoritarian control regimes, as it aims at designing and supporting transformative activities to change people and organizations. A clear implication of this is that the leader must participate in the change process. It is not a possible role for the leader to be a bystander of such a process. This leadership role implies that the leader must master the design of learning processes supporting change as well as being a person who masters leadership in a participative environment.

3 Participative Transformation – The Role of Technology and the Political Economy

In the previous chapters we emphasized that organizational change should be understood as a result of social learning processes and not as mechanical design of organizational machinery. However, change does not take place independent of conditions shaped by factors on the outside of organizational boundaries. First, organizations must be conceptualized as sociotechnical systems where technology is important for enabling or limiting different forms of organizing. The important role of technology and the option of choosing technology is absent in most literature on organizational change, but will be a main point in this book and specifically in this chapter. The potential in making technological choices in the same way as choosing organizational structures in organizational change processes is an essential position in the sociotechnical school. There is a striking ignorance in the literature on change and development on how the political economy will influence both organizational choices as well as opportunities for participatory design of change processes. To put it simply; what makes a good organizational change process in the US may not be possible or desirable in China, Norway or Egypt. We will not elaborate extensively on these issues, but rather point to how political and economic conditions should be attended to in order to be careful not to automatically transfer recipes for successful change between different political economies, without a thorough reflection on the particular conditions.

Technology as Constraining and Enabling Change

Classical organizational theory grew out of a period with technological optimism and determinism. New technology was uncritically seen as the driver of effective production and the role of people at work was to fulfil the potential of the technology. The first group of researchers to criticize this position and present an alternative thinking and approach was the sociotechnical school (STS). The sociotechnical thinking can be traced back (as discussed in the previous chapter) to the Tavistock Institute of Human Relations in London. Following the Second World War, this environment was involved in the reconstruction of the British industrial base. Eric Trist and Ken Bamforth published the first sociotechnical study in 1951. The object of this study was to explain why productivity in the English mining industry decreased when new technology was introduced. The main discovery was that the new production technology ("The longwall method of coal getting") broke down social organization in such a way that the working conditions worsened and efficiency decreased. In short, the lesson learned from this study was that technology and organization must be seen as two closely integrated systems. Changes in one will affect the other.

The lesson for leadership of change is that in development work, limitations and opportunities in the technological system will affect possible choices regarding constructing a new organization. Consequently, an OD process is never just social, but also technological.

The work that Eric Trist initiated was continued by the Australian Fred Emery, and would eventually play an important part in the research-based development of sociotechnical thinking. Emery had a strong interest in systems theory approaches (Emery 1969, 1981), and he was quick to apply these perspectives to organizations. In short, an organization was understood as an interaction between systems. One way of seeing this would be a tripartite division between social, technological and administrative factors. Equally important was Emery's (1969) solid argumentation for understanding organizations as open systems. Consequently, an organization depended on what was imported (raw material, energy, people, and so on) and on the environment's systematic influence on the organizational transformation process and the export of commodities or services to the external world.

Two publications in particular discuss and analyse the system theoretical perspective. Fred Emery's work from 1959, *Characteristics of Socio-technical Systems*, was essential. It carries the striking subheading: "A critical review of the theories and facts about the effects of technological change on internal structure of work organizations; with special reference to the effects of higher mechanization and automation."

A typical feature of the sociotechnical tradition was that knowledge was developed through research that addressed pertinent concrete problems and the research was focused on seeking practical solutions. This is also the reason that the Tavistock Institute became a key environment for the development of AR as a method (Greenwood and Levin 2007). In other words, the sociotechnical thinking developed a research strategy that united practical problem-solving and theoretical development. Systems theory thinking thus became important within sociotechnical thinking.

The second text was Emery and Trist's paper "The Causal Texture of Organizational Environments" published in 1965 in the journal *Human Relations*. In this article the impact of the environment upon organizational functioning was discussed and analysed and became a canon within this tradition. The essential point in this article is a discussion of organizations as open systems, and that different types of environments set different requirements to an organization's design. For example, organizations whose environment is stable and whose markets are relatively unchanging usually benefit from having a rigid organizational structure "geared" toward efficiency and stability. Typical examples are mass-producing industries that use assembly lines in production. On the other hand, companies whose markets are dynamic and turbulent have to find an organizational structure that is flexible and adaptable.

Sociotechnical principles for organizational design included structuring task dependencies and locating decision-making authority to the people who do the job. These principles led to the development of autonomous work groups, which in the last decades have been gaining ground under the label *team organization*. Further, STS focuses on organizational flexibility based on the principle of "redundancy of functions" (Trist 1981), aiming to make the organization more robust to changes (or resilient, which is the more popular contemporary term). This means that "disturbances" such as employee absence and production problems can be handled more smoothly because the workers were competent in more than one job and hence could take another job if needed. The alternative was redundancy of tasks, which implied that idle workers were called to help. If the work group was multi-skilled (redundancy of functions) they could handle the disturbance by themselves.

Another important design principle that originated from the STS camp was "minimum critical specification" (Herbst 1977). Herbst's point was to minimize rigid and detailed work descriptions. This would leave much room for the workers' choices and opportunities to create new and better work processes. Indeed, this is the core argument for establishing participative processes for change and development of organizations.

There are only fragments of texts within the STS tradition that explicitly deal with a theory of social change, but the researchers devoted quite a lot of intellectual energy to understanding and developing a praxis that would lead to organizational change. This praxis in change evolved from an expert-driven approach in the early experimental designs to a more participative approach where the researchers just supported participative design processes. STS was the first strand of thinking in organization theory to discuss "large scale change" as a part of its foundation. Central scholars like Eric Trist and Fred Emery developed insight into the dissemination of innovation (see, for example, Emery and Oeser 1958).

On the other hand, the praxis of STS has been epochal. A joint optimization (good fit) of social system and technology was the desired outcome and this "optimization" would mandate participation from the involved actor in order to find the point of joint optimization. Accordingly, the idea that it would be possible to form the best solution a priori was discarded.

Fundamental in sociotechnical thinking was a research grounded approach to what constituted good or preferable working conditions. Early sociotechnical theorists (particularly Eric Trist and Fred Emery) held that humanistic psychology could deliver perspectives on what were key factors in a good job. Further, Thorsrud and Emery (1970) refer to the creation of these ideas as essential to transforming the workplace. These work requirements were formulated as follows (our formulation of perspectives, in the Norwegian industrial democracy programme, based on Thorsrud and Emery 1970: 19–23):

1. the need for a minimum of variation in work;

2. the need to be able to learn during work; that is, on the job;

3. the need to be able to make work-related decisions of importance for the work performed;

4. the need for a certain amount of mutual respect between the humans involved;

5. the need to experience a relation between work and what is considered of value in society;

6. the need to see the job as compatible with a desirable future.

These psychological work requirements were then converted into a set of 11 principles for transforming jobs (Thorsrud and Emery 1970: 20–22; our translated summary):

1. a meaningful pattern of tasks that give each job the sense of a single overall task;

2. optimum length of work cycle;

3. some scope for setting standards of quantity and quality of production and suitable feedback of knowledge about results;

4. the inclusion in the job of some of the auxiliary and preparatory tasks;

5. the tasks included in the job should entail some degree of care, skill, knowledge or effort that is worthy of respect in the community;

6. the job should make some perceivable contribution to the utility of the product for the consumer;

7. provision for interlocking tasks, job rotation or psychological proximity where there is a necessary interdependence of jobs;

8. provision for interlocking tasks, job rotation or psychological proximity where the individual jobs do not make an obvious perceivable contribution to the utility of the end-product;

9. where a number of jobs are linked together by interlocking tasks or job rotation, they should be grouped;

10. provision of channels of communication so that the minimum requirements of the workers can be fed into the design of new jobs at an early stage;

11. provision of channels of promotion to supervisor rank that are sanctioned by the workers.

Based on this list, group-based organization of work was a solution that made it possible to realize many of the principles for creation of good jobs that would satisfy the psychological work requirements. This is probably the reason why "semi-autonomous" work groups turned out to be so prominent in sociotechnical thinking because the groups proved useful as building blocks in organized activity.

In a narrow understanding, sociotechnical thinking is a field of knowledge which is particularly geared to the interaction between technology and organization. In addition, sociotechnical transformation of organizations was based on democratic values. Solutions should at least contribute to a higher degree of influence and democracy in the workplace by creating participative change processes.

The Political Economy as a Supportive or Restrictive Factor for Change

We use "political economy" as a rather general description of the political arrangement of social and political institutions, legislations and traditions that condition the organization of working life. Politics and economy can constrain or enable change activities at company level, and the political economy varies quite a lot between countries. An example close at hand is to reflect upon how a feasible change activity in the US might not be possible in Northern Europe. The function and power of trade unions are different, the willingness to work collectively on problem solving is different and the expectations regarding participation and democracy at work might be hugely different.

One concrete example is to compare the principles of organizing and change from the Norwegian industrial democracy project (Thorsrud and Emery 1970) with the more recent popularity of flattened hierarchies and team-based organizing. In the industrial democracy project in the 1960s, a very central principle behind organizational design was to improve jobs and increase possibilities for participation and democracy. The semiautonomous work groups that were invented were central to achieving this. These organizational innovations were "exported," although slowly, to Sweden, US and Japan, but took very different forms as the interest in industrial democracy waned. The downplaying of the democratic issue made ideas on semiautonomous work groups transformed into teams, which was easily accommodated in the political economy in countries where work-life democracy had a significant meaning.

A second example relates to the lean production system – the concept that emerged in the wake of the MIT-based International Automobile Project and the publication by Womack et al. (1990) *The Machine that Changed the World*. The main thrust of this movement was to reconstruct Western production systems based on Japanese lean models. The Japanese political economy with a high degree of accepted authoritarian structures created the backdrop for the shaping of lean in Japan, but when transferred to North Western countries, the lack of strict societal authority made the direct copying of Japanese lean difficult. Where it was successfully applied, the whole conceptualization was adjusted to the local political, economic and societal reality.

Without trying to make an exhaustive list of factors in the political economy that will potentially impact organizational change projects, we suggest the following to be very important:

The Power, Legitimacy and Role of Workers' Unions

If the role of unions is introduced into discussions on organizational change, the initial arguments and positions in the discussion will be very different dependent upon what political economies the participants have as their reference. In the social democracies in Northern Europe it is hard to see that change processes might be feasible unless unions are heavily involved. In everyday life of mature industrial companies in these countries, management and union leaders will engage informally and almost continuously in discussions about challenges and concerns, and what might be possible solutions. The basis is that the parties accept that the others represent sometimes different interests and sometimes the same interests. Wage negotiations are localized to particular periods in time and particular situations, while discussions about developing profitable businesses are otherwise on the agenda. It is also evident in these North-European economies that unions and employers have developed agreement for mutual support for OD at the company level. In other countries, the hostilities between unions and management are so pronounced that unions in no way become a legitimate part of change processes. While employers see unions as a threat to long-term business opportunities, the unions see employers as totally without concern for their employees' situation. Obviously, these two different conditions would create very different points of departure for participation in change processes.

The Role of State Institutions in Shaping Conditions for Change

The state can influence conditions for change in different ways, from issuing legislation to direct economic intervention in work life. The state could be involved in the wage negotiations through supporting health and social benefits or through special agreements in public pension systems. In some countries state legislation regulates very strictly how jobs might be designed and how accountability is established in organizations. Change processes may also be regulated; that is, that employees have particular rights to participate in change processes that influence job content or their conditions of employment. In other countries such legislation is obviously totally absent and such concerns are only established as company policies. In political economies where regulations promote participation this would hugely support local initiatives. In some economies the state is even a direct supporter of specific change initiatives through giving access to facilitating competence integrated in public programmes that support business development.

Values and Traditions

Established industrial practices for participation will not only develop competence in participatory change, but also build mutual trust toward future change processes, as well as an expectation from involved parties as to how company leaders will handle future challenges and changes. Again, this varies between companies, as we have already argued when it comes to the more formal roles of state and unions. Social values and norms that are established at the societal level, in particular industries and in larger companies, will create a very particular starting point for local change processes, whether or not participatory approaches to change will be seen as feasible or desirable.

Organizational change does not take place in a vacuum but will be subject to influence by the social and material (technology) environment of the local company.

Participation – The Material Context and the Political Economy

Let us return to the industrial experiments of creating new organizations based on sociotechnical principles and in a direction of a more democratic working life. As more experience was gained, it became evident that the *process* of introducing new organizational principles dominates the result. One cannot command democracy. It must be developed through participating in and experiencing a democratic process. In the perspective of workplace development, the argument is that a participatory organization must be developed through democratic processes.

This recognition was reached gradually through the experiences gained in the Norwegian industrial democracy programme. In the initial phases, the experiments were driven forward by experts in sociotechnical design. These researchers carried out an analysis of the organization, developed alternative ways of organizing work and were very active in the implementation of new solutions. The challenge was that the solutions were those of the experts, with little or no ownership by employees. This expert-driven change created a challenge in finding ways of utilizing the employees' insights and experience in the new organizational solutions, and made intensive training necessary in the implementation phase. On the other hand, it is clear that the sociotechnical solutions would not have come into being without deep commitment from experts.

The dilemma lies in how to bring expert knowledge into participatory development processes. A conceptualization of this challenge in this book is formulated in the co-generative model that is presented in the next chapter. The essential perspective of this model is to build a bridge between different strands of knowledge. In short, mutual learning in common arenas creates room for both expert-based knowledge and local insight.

4 Participative Change as Co-generative Learning

In previous chapters we have presented and discussed different positions in the fields of organizational theory and organizational change. The argument has favoured a theoretical position that conceptualizes everyday organizational practices as constitutive of what the organization is and can be. In addition, it is argued for an approach to organizational change that is based on involving its members in collective learning processes. In Chapters 5 and 6 theories and concepts of learning and participation will be discussed. In this chapter we will present a model for organizational change that shows how learning and participation are related. At the same time, the model should serve as a practical guidance for making knowledge-based decisions about how a particular development process could and should be organized and led.

The model is strongly influenced by participative AR, and in particular the co-generative learning model developed by Elden and Levin (1991) and Greenwood and Levin (1998, 2007). Co-generative learning has two major building blocks. First, it is grounded on how new knowledge is developed through concrete experimentation in order to solve practical problems. Second, it is founded on democratic values. The knowledge development and the change activity must support increased ability to control one's own situation.

Pragmatic philosophy serves as the conceptual fundament for the co-generative learning model as well as the model for participatory organizational change. One fundamental argument is that, in seeking knowledge, people participate in a holistic social and material context within which the knowledge is created (Skjervheim 1974). In other words, the knowledge generated and the actual learning are influenced by social position in the organization as well as material (that is, technological) conditions. Also, new knowledge is brought about through actively seeking solutions to the problem in focus. In pragmatic terms the essence is "to make an indeterminate situation determinate through active experimentation in a holistic situation to create warranted assertions" (Dewey 1991/1938). In simpler terms, there is no single factor that establishes new knowledge. A warranted assertion, that is, something that ends up as claiming to be true, is generated through successive experimentation that gradually makes the situation determined.

John Dewey (1859–1952) holds an exceptional position among pragmatic philosophers in contributing insights necessary to support arguments for the core processes in co-generative learning (participative change). Dewey had a significant interest in democracy which he considered to be an on-going collective process for social development and improvement that would impact all societal levels (Dewey 1991/1927). The educational system was especially important because it prepared the social actors through scholarship to participate in political processes. Democracy cannot be commanded but has to be learned through active participation in knowledge-generating processes. These arguments from Dewey constitute the foundation for the co-generative model, stating the reason why broad participation is fundamental and arguing for participation as an underpinning for a democratic learning process.

The Three Phases of Organizational Change

The change process can be divided into three phases. The change starts with a clarification of the direction and objectives for the development work. A common approach is to see this phase as a task for management levels, sometimes assisted by analysis or diagnosis shaped by outside experts. An obvious concern is that understanding and insight at managerial levels will not necessarily include what appears to be important to other members of the organization. Similarly, external experts rarely define the challenges in the same way as the employees in the organization. In a participatory development process it is therefore argued that employees who live with the problems on a daily basis should experience the initial analysis and conclusions about problem definitions as grounded also in their reality, and that their everyday work situation are included or addressed. The challenge in this first phase is to obtain and integrate the different views and knowledge. Joint discussions can provide learning opportunities that can create opportunities for new voices to be heard. Already the first phase of problem clarification has the character of co-generative learning by involving all the relevant actors.

The next phase is the start-up of the actual change process. In this phase, it is important to build a foundation for a long-term learning process. The process orientation rhetoric, without strong promises of quick fixes, may become a challenge in itself. Not many leaders or employees have personal experience of being involved in participatory change processes. For employees, years of experience of being controlled by others may need to be challenged and replaced with thinking where employees see themselves as actively engaged in shaping their own work conditions. For leaders, it may be a change from being in total detailed control to trusting the competence and business orientation of employees. A good rule of thumb in this initial phase is to find problems that can be addressed and resolved quickly, simply to create concrete and collective experiences in creating solutions that are visible and that matters.

The third phase in organizational change is to create a continuous learning spiral. The development is based on developing concrete solutions to problems and opportunities that leaders and participants in the organization identify as important. These solutions give rise to collective reflection processes that develop new insights, which provides the basis for new concrete organizational initiatives.

The learning process is cyclic. Reflection on one's own practice can contribute to direct improvements of practice, but it may also contribute to new practices, new frameworks of understanding and processes involving other participants and other fields of interaction.

Participative Change as Co-generative Learning

From a management perspective, organizational change is to design and lead learning processes. The essence is to structure the interaction between leaders and participants. The leadership implies designing learning opportunities that bring employees into a position to make good decisions acquired from this increased competence. These insights lead to concrete and practical change that subsequently generates knowledge resources to be activated at a later stage.

Co-generative learning is to integrate the communicative processes on various types of arenas in the same learning process. People who take active part in a change process and can participate on various arenas are accordingly enrolled in the overall collective learning process. Second, the co-generative learning model situates the leader or the change agent with their own integrity and still integrated with and deeply involved in the development process. A third element in the model is the emphasis on how learning is supported and enables the creation of common knowledge through solving concrete problems.

It is the knowledge developed through learning from concrete actions that is the "engine" in this change process. Accordingly, it is important to design arenas where participants can meet and learn together. Both leaders and employees are part of the same learning process and each participant contributes their particular competencies to the process. This is an important point because the participants and leaders have diverse positions and roles both in terms of ownership of problems and in opportunities to and responsibility for leading a change process.

There are two major learning loops in the model shown in Figure 4.1. The left side loop identifies to the involved employees their activity related to solving the concrete problem at hand. This activity will shape a reflection process that creates sustained learning relevant to everyday operation. At the same time, the leaders or change agents hook up to a learning process related

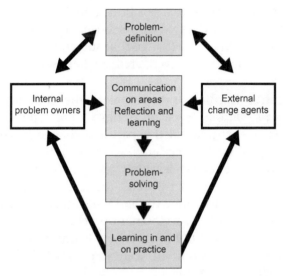

Figure 4.1   Participatory change as co-generative learning

to the practice of leading development and change. This is the right side loop and constitutes an important learning loop for the leader as well as for the organizational change practices.

Phases, Actors and Learning Loops

The change process has three distinct phases and they are integrated in the model. The first phase is given by the problem clarification, while the second and third phases follow the logic specified by the learning loops in the model. It is important to underscore that these two learning loops are both similar and different. Based on experiences gained through the change process, the participants engage in sensemaking processes within their own social and material context. These processes will in turn provide a basis for new input to the change process. In an ideal self-sustained learning process the left side (participants) will be in full control and the right hand side (change agents, leaders) will be wheeled off in the sense that their input is not necessary for the change activity

Problem Clarification

The first phase of any change process is to clarify the problem. This is a critical phase in all change work, particularly in processes depending on participation. The first problem clarification is in many ways a miniature change process. Actors learn to know each others' positions, develop an initial basis of trust and sketch out the first concrete actions and share learning. The work should result in an understanding of the problem, framed in such a way that it seems feasible to solve it. Trust must be established, and the foundation for this is built through the mutual learning process. The most important challenge in the problem clarification phase is to create a bridge that enables good communication between the potentially different initial perspectives held by leaders or outside facilitators and groups of participants. The first assignment is to a provide means of understanding the local insights organization members bring with them. At the same time, input from external actors (expert analysis, models and perspectives, customer voices, benchmarks, and so on) may open up new perspectives. The most fruitful problem clarification is established through a dialogue that allows different perspectives to be raised and challenged. In this encounter between different positions and perspectives, a foundation is laid for a shared understanding created through new meaning jointly understood.

There is always a variety of motives behind initiating change. There may be claims about quality, cost, productivity or culture. The important point is that there always exist many motives and interests in the different participating groups. In a process of change that is designed to be run by the participants' active involvement, it is an absolute condition that the goals for all involved are acceptable and legitimate. Accordingly, it is necessary to have an initial clarification and a development of a consensus by the involved parties. Different motives and goals must be transformed into mutually-accepted objectives and strategies for the change process.

Several clarifications must be made simultaneously. First, it is imperative to involve representatives of the groups that are most affected in order to develop local understanding of a problem. The leader of the change process must facilitate communication and problem-solving that can help to develop a mutually acceptable frame of reference for the change process to come. At the same time, the leader will have or develop an independent understanding of the initial situation. The purpose is not create a "truth" to evaluate others' arguments against, but rather to stand forward as an actor with explicit and clear arguments in dialogues with different parties in the organization. Skills in organizational analysis, coupled with an understanding of how the discussions on problem clarification could be facilitated, are important competencies for leading change in this phase. The process leaders have to choose work forms that fit the actual context, taking into consideration the people involved, the material and the economic conditions. The quality of the process depends on how the participants are able to see alternative approaches before choosing the path for future work. A good recommendation is to play with alternative plans, processes and solutions in an early phase, instead of making early premature conclusions. It is often fruitful to choose an initial starting point where it is fair to assume that it will be easy to get the first positive results. "Quick rewards" have a high motivating effect, which can often be important in order to mobilize commitment to the change process.

Planning and Designing Arenas for Joint Reflection and Learning

Planning in organizational change implies arrangement of processes and not "engineering" of results. In participatory change it is important to escape from the classical organization division between actors who simply decide and plan for others' actions and those who merely contribute to achieving the goals. Planning is to design arenas for dialogue and learning. Any arena will have its own material and social characteristics that limit or enable how people can work and learn. The leader (or external change agent) must be acquainted with alternative arenas and how these effect participation and communication. Shaping and facilitating learning processes in arenas represents the most important challenges for the process leader.

Arenas can take many forms. First, every meeting is potentially a learning arena. Even in a large meeting dominated by one-way communication, it will develop certain forms of joint reflection and learning because attendees pick up and discuss input from the monologue. Yet this is one of the less fruitful forums of mutual learning. At the other end of the spectrum are group-based activities where it is quite easy to get people actively engaged as learners. However, there is no single best way to design a learning arena. The choice will be based on context-sensitive judgment. What problem seems to be central, who should participate and what is the relevant organizational environment? An important condition for managing change processes is to choose from a repertoire of possible arena designs. Too often, consulting practices specialize in one specific method, which results in use of the same approach regardless of the actual challenges. In Part II of this book we provide examples of arenas and work forms that vary both with respect to working methods and potential outcomes. It is a requirement in leading participatory change that the leader understands the qualities of different arenas and work forms and, based on this knowledge, is able to recognize or design arenas for fruitful learning processes.

Designing good arenas for learning is thus the key to a successful change process. Leading the change process is to obtain an understanding of the specific organization, its operation and challenges. This can only be achieved through good contact with people from different parts of the organization.

Problem-solving and Reflection

The results of the change work materialize through improved ability to identify and handle specific challenges in more efficient ways. "The proof of the pudding" is the improved ability to master problematic issues and create results. This capacity is not only reflected in concrete problem-solving, but also in how the organization is better able to manage its own learning processes. Results will and must always be measured in both the short and long terms.

Learning processes in the first phase will result in concrete solutions that are implemented. These experiments reflect the prior learning and give rise to important experiences for further processes. The results, whether positive or negative, are the basis for further development. A first step in this learning process is to systematically detect data that can identify whether the actions have produced desired outcomes. When it comes to measuring intermediate results, it is yet again important to recognize the difference between a top-down control approach and a bottom-up participative approach. In a top-down process, data and measurements will inevitably be seen as a control regime to evaluate performance. This will in turn produce defensive strategies to either avoid measurements or make results look better than they really are. In a participatory approach built on learning as change, measurement should be seen as feedback that is necessary to understand the terrain we are manoeuvring in. It is important in such a change process to create consensus that it is through the systematic "experiments" that one can develop the organization, which also implies the possibility of making mistakes.

The continuous learning process in the organizational work is simply a sequence of:

1. collective reflection in order to develop alternatives for action;

2. experimentation to achieve desired goals;

3. collective reflection on achieved results;

4. separate learning loops, related to participants and leaders of change;

5. feedback and new learning on the shared learning arenas.

This is a continual learning spiral. An important process objective is to gradually reduce the influence of the leader or change agent. Leaders or change agents are key actors who initiate and lead the first phase in the participatory change process. Managing change processes is ideally expected to be taken over by the problem owners in any learning organization.

Individual Reflection Processes for "Participants" and "Leaders"

Organizational change is conceptualized as a collective learning process, yet the different parties in a change process will need to reflect on and think through the processes, outcomes and goals, based upon their own unique roles, interests and positions. Groups of participants shape their own understanding about if and how they participate in change. Leaders of change make the same kind of reflections; "based on experiences so far, how can we best proceed?" In any change process it is important and natural that involved parties continuously assess whether what they do and how they do is useful and important.

A particular concern is of course situations where processes breaks down, when leaders want to call off the designed process or participants no longer want to participate. A practical recommendation for this type of situation is that the design of a participative process also involves creating an explicit agreement that defines how conflicts should be handled and eventually how the process may be terminated. If a change process is in trouble, it should be handled in such a way that the parties learn why the problems arose and what the others' positions are. One option is the 60–60 principle. It takes only 60 seconds to declare that one no longer believe in the progress of the process, but it must be a requirement that the parties also spend 60 minutes to develop mutual understanding of why the process has not progressed as desired. This mutual clarification is not intended to create solutions to the breach or the conflict (that it took 60 seconds to convey), but to ensure mutual learning and understanding, that may of course also be crucial for future work.

For leaders of the change process, time for reflection on role and experiences is important to ensure the continued learning that provides the basis for improved leadership (or change agent) practice. The experience gained from the change process must be transformed into learning in such a way that the process leaders become reflective practitioners.

From Planned Change to Ongoing Change Process

The co-generative learning model of participatory change builds on a basic idea that learning and development are implemented in an interplay between participants and leaders who mutually engage in identifying problems and challenges, create workable solutions and learn about both problems, solutions and new opportunities along the way. Leadership of change is the ability and the capacity to initiate and to bring about those learning processes, which both solves concrete everyday problems but also builds a long-term learning potential in the organization.

Leading change processes must be moved to the zone of everyday work in an organization. Every leader must have the skills to shape and support the necessary learning and developmental processes needed for short-term problem-solving, but must also be able to build strategic capacity for long-term survival. Change leadership is not necessarily to be understood as "Leadership" with a capital L, but practising change leadership in daily work is a skill that has to be integrated into all management activity. We will elaborate further on leadership roles and competences in this perspective in Chapter 7.

The Philosophical- and Value-based Foundation of Co-generative Learning

The co-generative model relies on joint employee and management engagement in seeking solutions to concrete problems. The pragmatic foundation implies that the participants in the change process are actively involved in creating new solutions to particular problems. What emerges then as knowledge from such a process? What is usually considered as "knowledge" in everyday language is what can be stated explicitly. This is knowledge that can be verbalized, discussed and communicated. This is the kind of knowledge that Gilbert Ryle (1949) in his book *The Concept of Mind* identified as "knowing what". On the other hand, this explicit knowledge does not contain all the insights that are generated in the learning process. Ryle (1949) coined another form of knowing as "know how," which is a form of knowledge that is identified through a person's ability and skills to act in practice. In other words "know how" is not what we talk about, but it is knowledge that is engraved in the ability to act concretely.

The contextuality that is engraved in all knowledge is a major argument forwarded by Wittgenstein (1953). He argues that language games between participants always take place within social and material frameworks that generate interpretation and understanding of what verbal utterances means. This position is the reason for generating situated knowledge processes not only because they would become meaningful for involved actors, but also because these process are participative and genuinely democratic. In a co-generative learning process "know how" would be accessible for participants through the active involvement in solving concrete problems.

Everyday knowledge is the central perspective in Polanyi's (1966) book *The Tacit Dimension*. He develops a perspective that there is a form of human knowledge that is hidden and only accessible through acting. In this respect it coincides with Ryle's "know how". The "tacit" knowing is a human capacity that manifests itself through the ability to act skilfully in ways that we cannot explain with words. The basic argument is exemplified by showing how children are able to speak grammatically correctly without having any intellectual understanding of grammar as an explicit phenomenon. In the same way, a human would develop skills that enable problem-solving without necessarily being able to put into words why or how problems were actually solved.

In any organizational activity all three knowledge forms are generated, and the co-generative learning process take this as an important premise. All participants should have access to the (common) knowledge that is created. A good process would result in practical solutions that are both participative and transparent. New knowledge would be engraved in current practice and it would simultaneously shape the platform for research-based analysis and knowledge dissemination.

How Can and Should Ideas and Solutions Be Assessed?

An important question to raise is what is the quality of what is experienced, learned and held as knowledge? What knowledge is "true"? What is the better solution? The best criterion if a specific solution fulfils expectations is whether the "solution" solves the problem in focus. In this respect, the essential criterion is if the solution "works". This is again the basis upon which it is possible to conclude in pragmatic philosophical terms that the knowledge engraved in the working solutions becomes warranted assertions.

There will not always be a consensus among different levels or units in an organization on how to interpret a result or to apply the same model to explain a particular phenomenon. Solutions would be preferred by some groups simply because they are beneficial for their particular interests. It is not necessarily so that consensus in interpreting results among participating group is a fundamental prerequisite. It is possible for employees to live with results from a developmental process that only partially serves their interests. On the other hand, it would be important for the participants to understand how the results fulfil different groups' particular interests.

Participative Change in a Democratic Society

Finally, we will reflect on some large perspectives given by the co-generative model. This model for organizational change is framed on a high degree of participation. This will be explored further in Chapter 6, but we will in particular point to three arguments as important.

The pragmatic philosophical arguments for co-generative learning as a model for organizational change make it natural to seek support in Dewey's thinking on democracy. He argued for the fundamental importance of democracy in a civilized society and as an ethical ideal for humankind (1966/1916, 1991/1927).

Participation is emphasized as a premise for the democratic ideal that supports the co-generative learning model. The argument for this position can be drawn from Pateman's (1970) book *Participation and Democratic Theory*. Pateman shows that there are alternatives to the representative democracy where people elect a governing elite to rule for a specific period and where democracy is assured through peoples' rights and duty to elect their political leaders. Pateman argued for an alternative and supplementary form. The point would be to create democracy by giving individuals space and opportunity to impact and control their immediate life conditions, either in working life or in local neighbourhoods. The underlying idea in participative democracy is to build on engagement and involvement from the citizens and at the same time prepare the ground for active participation. It is vital that the participants can make decisions based on their own perspectives and priorities.

Co-generative Learning, Research Method and Work Forms

What is the relationship between research methods in social science and work forms in co-generative learning? Work forms represent a practice in designing arenas and learning processes to support development. A work form will accordingly be a concrete "tool" directed toward creating change and development in an organization. On the other hand, work forms are not methods as those are defined in social science. A method in social science is a transparent methodology that embraces construction of data and how to analyse the data in order to make warranted assertions built on professional knowledge.

Work forms and social science methodology are linked because social science methodology is applied in order to systematize and interpret results or problems emerging in a developmental process. Greenwood and Levin (2007) differentiate between AR strategy, work forms and social science techniques. The AR strategy incorporates the basic structuration of problem definition, common learning on a communicative arena and development of concrete and practical solutions. A work form is chosen to design a communicative arena that clarifies the actual communication process, learning opportunities and participants. The social science techniques represent the total arsenal of professional methodological approaches. In Part II we will elaborate on different work forms.

Participation – A Cornerstone in Organizational Change

This model for organizational change is framed on a high degree of participation. Three arguments are important.

First, a practical argument is grounded in economic and practical effectiveness just because resistance to change would be less as employees have been actively involved in developing the solutions they will use (Greenberg 1975, Levin 1984). Greenberg in particular makes this point as he shows that interest in participation varies between different groups in an organization. Pragmatic use of participation dominates management echelons, while trade unionists see participation as a political right.

Second, participation in the co-generative model is grounded in participative democracy. It is built on values that employees should have opportunities to direct and impact their own working conditions. A democratic practice in work life can therefore also be seen as the embryo for spreading democracy to other arenas in society.

Third, the co-generative learning has the potential of democratizing the knowledge generating process in society at large. Participative involvement by all in shaping practical solutions, in addition to being actively engaged in the meaning construction process related to the emerging practical solutions, can create the basis for knowledge construction based on their own interests. Participation in political and economic activity is very important, but the core is the democratic process of creating new knowledge. Hopefully, co-generative learning can be useful for some initial steps on the road to increased democracy.

5   Learning and Knowledge

We hold in this book that organizational change results from learning processes. It's a simple and clear position, but it is also the seed of controversies. This perspective emerges strongly from our grounding position that change in organizations can only occur through individual enactment. Any authority might mandate the changes, but change will only take place when the individuals alter their action repertoire (we will identify this as the local action theory later in this chapter). Change can never bypass the individual's concrete decision to obey the new expectations. Therefore all organizational change involves every employee and thus de-facto mandate participation as inseparable from any change process.

Understanding learning in organizations is therefore important. The chapter is introduced with a discussion on learning in organizations. Then the notion of learning organizations is introduced. Learning organizations have received a lot of attention over the last two decades and the focus of this has been on the qualities of organizations that enable learning. Finally, learning is seen through the lens of knowledge theory, relating these processes to the conceptualization of knowledge and knowledge management in the late 1990s.

Theories of Action

"The organization" is often, by theorists as well as by laymen, understood as a structure that exists independent of its members. This so-called "structural" perspective invites an understanding of organizational change and development focuses on analysing, redesigning and then implementing new structures. Human action is seen as a direct consequence of structure. This book holds a "constructivist" position in which people produce their organizational realities, including what is conceived as structures, through their everyday activities. It is the action and social interaction in everyday work that constitutes what is understood as "the organization". Formal descriptions like charts, handbooks, formal procedures and so on may communicate internally and externally what the organizational practices are *intended* to be and how they are intended to be performed, but it is actual practices and not their formal descriptions that constitute the organization.

Actions in organizations are guided by the members' understanding of how the organization works, which norms and values apply, how responsibilities are delegated, how members interact and affect other organizational members, how the technology works and how the organization is controlled. This understanding is learned. When employees enter a new work situation, they have little insight into this organizational reality and a modest understanding of jobs, expectations and relationships. Learning is achieved while working with colleagues. There is obviously much that is impossible to learn from "outside" work or before generating experiences. The individual has worked in a social community. A new social reality is learned, which will be guiding focus, decisions, norms, expectations, understanding of procedures, technology, and so on. This understanding is what Argyris and Schön (1978) call "theories of action", precisely because they are "local theories" that form the basis for actions.

How is it possible to make sense of one's own and other people's theories of action? Partly, theories of action are explicit. If someone asked you *how* and *why* you do a particular job, you would obviously have something to say about it. You would present your *espoused* theory of action, the explicit description of what you do and what understanding and principles guide what you do. You may even present what you understand to be the given or dominant thinking about this work in the organization, as part of the *organizational* theory espoused. However, if someone observed you working for a while, it is possible they would form a different understanding of what you really do and of the principles that guide your actions. This is the *theories-in-use* in the organization. There may be differences between what is said when describing the work and the organization, and what could be observed about the actual work done. There may be good reasons for that. First, behaviour may have been routinized over time and become action-based knowledge of a kind that cannot be articulated (tacit knowledge is discussed later in this chapter). Second, if asked, the individual might want to present practices as one would like them to be, not as they actually are. The important practical implication is to be aware of this potential difference between actual practices (theories-in-use) and what people may *state* as their practices (espoused theory).

Individual Learning versus Organizational Learning

Individual learning capabilities is necessary, but not sufficient, prerequisite for an organization to learn. It is required because organizational tasks are unavoidably carried out by the individuals in the organization. If no individuals have changed what they do or developed their capacity to do something else, the organization will not do anything new, nor improve its potential for change. On the other hand, learning at the individual level does not automatically create changes at the organizational level. A much-used example is the manager or co-worker who, through an external course, gains experiences, reflections and ideas that create a foundation for entirely new practices, but who is then met by the old organizational life when they return. Others may perceive the good ideas as diffuse or remote, and irrelevant for their work situation. Individual learning does not create changes at the organizational level because an organization is not an individual phenomenon, but a collective and relational. The organization changes through collective and interlocked transformation.

So far the discussion has been on theories of action at the individual level. However, the most interesting part is to understand the existence and relevance of organizational or collective theories of action. Over time, clear understanding is established between organizational members of what is important or unimportant, of how tasks and authority are actually distributed between people and between departments, of how particular systems and technologies work, and of how certain actions will cause negative and positive reactions. These are experiences gained by the individuals in the organization and they are shared to such an extent that they represent the organization's theory of action. If it is possible to state that action theories or theories-in-use can be collective, and learning is defined as changes in theories of action, it will also be meaningful to claim that organizations can learn. Changes in theory of action (theory-in-use) embody organizational learning.

Organizational learning requires that members actually participate in the learning process, and it cannot be delegated to a few on behalf of the community. Sometimes people participate in collective reflections that produce new understanding and solutions; at other times the collective learning is restricted to adapting to changes that are communicated through the established organizational hierarchy. However, if people are to change what they do, this must be learned, and the more the actual changes depend upon people's skills and commitment, it has to be built on active and real participation. Organized work is collective interaction. Therefore, the understanding that builds and develops organized activities must be created in the same collective.

Defence Mechanisms, Model I and II

In literature on organizational learning, there is a clear difference between early works from the late 1970s and contributions from the 1990s. Chris Argyris has traced mechanisms that explain why learning does *not* occur with a particular attention to defensive mechanisms. An early and much-cited article that points out processes that inhibit learning is entitled "Skilled Incompetence" (Argyris 1986). The vital perspective is how some forms of communication are at the same time incompetent (because they inhibit learning and improvement) and skilled (because individuals have practised these forms of communication extensively from early school years). These "skills" typically make it difficult to openly address challenges and to evaluate results, and instead foster communication that is typically ambiguous and filled with "mixed messages". The defensive strategy for the skilled mixed messenger is to make sure that no matter what happens, they can exit without any blame for negative results while at the same time be seen as responsible for what goes well. The particular relevance of these insights is that they point out that even if arenas for dialogue are designed, the communication and the quality of the learning processes may be shaped by the strategies and the "culture" developed in past processes. We have to learn to learn.

Argyris points out that there are ideal types of thinking (or theories-in-use) that strongly affect the ability to learn (see, for example, Argyris et al. 1985). He names these established patterns as Model I and Model II. In *Model I* thinking, focus is on formulating one's own goals and fighting to achieve these unilaterally. It is natural and important in this "bull fight" to suppress emotions and appear cool and rational. *Model II*, on the contrary, is based on a fundamental assumption that ideas and good arguments are what count and not who launches them. If a person is open minded and trusts other people, then they will respond openly towards other members of the organization. The emphasis is typically on assessing the validity of information and that decisions are supported by reasonable arguments. Actors may of course have strong views and it is accordingly important to create an organizational (social) openness so that others can challenge both data and interpretations. The dialogue between members of the organization determines what is valid and important.

The contrast between Model I and Model II behaviour is valuable if the aim is to recognize and understand particular patterns of communication and behaviour in organizational hierarchies. The two dominant models are also products of past learning, and that it is possible to develop good or bad climates for learning. Is it assumed, when employees are invited to discuss future opportunities and needs for change, that they really are adversaries? Or is the belief that they share the interest for quality, results and a positive future that is held by other members in the organization? In particular, leaders play a very important role in setting the standards of communication and for deciding whether defence or openness is the dominant approach to challenges that may arise.

Single-loop and Double-loop Learning

Members in organizations develop collective theories of action, shared norms, values and action theories that promote particular collective work forms. These may be seen as shaped through responses to internal or external demands or needs. The collective sensemaking of frequent encounters would be remembered, and creates a shared anticipation of responses that shapes collective actions performed without discussions or surprises. Argyris and Schön (1996) call this our "collective action strategies", while March and Simon (1958) used the term "programs" and Nelson and Winter (1982) "routines" to express much the same.

These processes of collective activities run smoothly as long as action strategies produce expected results. Reflections and inquiries are not initiated without reason. Processes that may lead to learning will be triggered only when the action strategies no longer produce the desired results. Following Argyris and Schön's conceptual scheme, two types of learning may occur. *Single-loop learning* is a one-dimensional corrective learning that is easily introduced and accepted. This occurs when goals and values are held unquestioned and the intention is to improve action strategies. For example, organizational members may want to improve health and safety in the organization by keeping people informed about important knowledge and principles as well as about internal safety routines and performance. As long as this strategy produces the desired safety results, there will be no significant change. If accidents happen or the statistics show negative results, how would the reaction be? A single-loop response will typically use the same type of strategies (informing) but amplify the efforts.

A double-loop response, on the other hand, will question the way members view the problem. Should a totally different approach to learning be applied? While single-loop responses stress the need to do things right, double-loop also questions whether the right things are done. Raising such fundamental questions is difficult. The core query is to what extent it is possible for employees in an organization to learn as an integrated element of daily work. Argyris and Schön (1978, 1996) discussed this primarily in relation to Model I and II. How can fundamental reasoning about integrated forms of action that build transparency and active searching for improvements be stimulated? These processes are fundamental to good learning. In the 1990s, a discussion about whether it was possible to cultivate reasoning and praxis in organizations to an extent that it could be identified as a "learning organization".

Action theory provides a different approach to understanding organization and change than earlier behaviouristic theories. Mainstream organizational theory largely regarded the organization and people as mechanical parts that were controlled through insight from a specific standpoint. Argyris and Schön's (1978, 1996) contribution was to get on the "inside" of day-to-day activity in the organization to be able to support an with understanding on how practice depends on local insights.

On the other hand, there is considerable similarity between this approach and AR. One difference is that while Argyris and Schön's contribution is directed at understanding local development processes (or often the lack of such) in organizations, AR is also concerned with the potential role of research in the development of organizations. Argyris and Schön (particularly Argyris) had their primary experience from communication and learning in and between different levels of management, while AR is explicitly directed at groups that ordinarily do not have a strong voice or are able to control their own working conditions. AR is value-driven, while Argyris and Schön adhere more to a position where they advocate that a knowledge-seeking process will promote good values and a better society, simply because the enlightened person will be good. Both schools of thought argue the importance of focusing on the processes that challenge accepted everyday knowledge. Argyris and Schön's contribution has been influential in academic discourses within AR in much the same way that the discourses of AR have made important contributions to key areas of OD.

In a summarizing perspective that guides development within action science, Argyris et al. (1985) particularly emphasizes the following:

- Action science should produce valid knowledge of how individuals and social systems can design and implement their desires in everyday life.

- A complete description of a reality must include a description of this universe's potential to change itself. (Here, they point out that as a researcher, one has a normative view of what a good society is, but that this view must always be actively exposed to empirical testing.)

- That all intentional action is based on reasoning and that this reasoning is often difficult to change.

- Action science is concerned with how people interpret experiences, and with the connection between understanding and one's own actions.

- Action science's contribution to understanding actions should be directly useful to acting individuals and organizations.

Argyris and Schön (1978; 1996) have created a conceptual bedrock for the understanding of learning in organizations. In addition, Chris Argyris has written a series of texts that shapes a perspective on how and why learning processes are impeded in organizations. It is particularly important to study communication and internalized sensemaking patterns. Donald Schön has delivered important research contributions to close the connection between practice and reflection. Schön is a central contributor to the increased awareness of the importance of practice-based knowledge, and to understanding learning processes that happen in shared reflection and practical work.

From Organizational Learning to Learning Organizations

While Argyris and Schön primarily conceptualized organizational learning processes, Peter Senge's *The Fifth Discipline* (1990) made a contribution to understanding which skills should be developed in the organization in order to increase the capacity to learn. This was not something Senge pulled out of the blue; neither was it an individual contribution from Senge. The bestseller's prehistory was based on interactions between industrial and academic environments. Arie de Geus, who wrote the book *The Living Company* (1997), is attributed with paternity of the concept of "learning organization". He belonged to the upper management echelon of the oil company Royal Dutch Shell. He was responsible for the company's operations in an unstable African country and was irritated because the company's extensive planning department was not particularly useful. This department was seemingly working on a lot of important things, but whenever site managers needed their help, there was little help forthcoming. De Geus vented his frustration, and in return he was challenged to lead the planning department.

Royal Dutch Shell and De Geus initiated cooperation with the research group led by the renowned cybernetics professor Jay Forrester at MIT. Forrester wanted to use cybernetics to understand and model both economic relationships and human behaviour. He had already provoked macro economists by claiming that his models could predict the development of a national economy better than the existing economic models. His contact with Shell provided opportunities to find new applications for ideas from cybernetics.

Peter Senge's (1990) book was a formidable success and a precursor for several books and professional networks that gathered academics, companies and consultants around this field throughout the 1990s. The message in *The Fifth Discipline* is that for an organization to be a "learning organization" the members must cultivate five disciplines. Among these, the fifth discipline, *systems thinking* and *system dynamics*, was the book's original contribution. The argument was that the world is systemic, and that the relationship between an organization and its environment can be modelled in such a way that causes change in one area to have large effects that we are not aware of somewhere else. Without this understanding, we run a risk of using unnecessary resources to solve problems that might have simple causes, or that the solution to a problem causes even greater difficulties in another area. In the book, Senge (1990) claims that there is a tendency to model simple linear relationships, while we lose the dynamic connections. Consequently, inefficient solutions are developed because they are based on flawed understanding. Therefore, developing mindsets, theories and tools that use insights from systems thinking is presented as the main challenge and opportunity for the field and for the modern manager.

"Single-loop" and "double-loop" learning are cybernetic concepts borrowed from systems theory, and conceptualize different learning loops in organizational praxis. Peter Senge's (1990) popular book *The Fifth Discipline* made systems theory virtually part of everyday language in corporate management and professional circles in the 1990s. The ambitions of the book were not to describe learning in organizations per se, but to understand what competencies or disciplines should be developed in order to support efficient learning. The five disciplines that Senge describes as fundamental are: systems thinking; personal mastery; mental models; building shared vision and team learning (Senge 1990: 5–10).

Personal mastery is about the development of one's own vision for work in the organization, as well as focusing energy toward learning and development. The learning organization can only become a reality if individuals really want to and are able to learn. *Mental models* are the cognitive understanding that leaders and employees have of how the organization functions. They represent, therefore, an understanding of how the organization functions (largely overlapping what we have called theories of action). A central challenge is to bring forth mental models and make them objects of common reflection. *Building shared vision* involves creating processes that develop a shared vision among the members of the organization. The basic challenge is to contribute to a shared direction. *Team learning* emphasizes the potential in using teams as organizational units as well as instruments for learning and development. Team learning becomes a collective phenomenon, where the interaction between team members is both a condition for and a consequence of learning. *System thinking* was the fifth discipline that Senge devoted most of the book to. It focuses on understanding how different elements and processes in an organization, and between the organization and its environment, are connected as a functional whole. Systems thinking is not primarily a tool for the expert who would analyse and then present to others what kind of problems they have and potential solutions. More important is that the problem-solving potential depends on how much is understood of how the different parts, strategies and actors are linked together in time and space. What may be a solution to a problem in one location may cause major problems in another location, or in the future. Therefore systems thinking is important at all levels and for all employees. What may seem like a huge problem, may find its solution in small changes. In engaging in shaping effective strategies for future collective results, one must develop a broad understanding of how organizational units and practices are connected in a systemic whole.

Knowledge Management and the Re-introduction of Tacit Knowing

In the beginning of the 1990s, knowledge management emerged as a new function in corporate staffs, as a professional service and as a new field of research. The dominant knowledge management approach was to search for new options for storing and retrieving large amounts of information, based on the assumption that such systems would create well-functioning corporate memory and support the spreading of important knowledge across organizational boundaries. This objectivistic assumption about the nature of knowledge was obviously quite problematic; storing and spreading "information" did not imply storing and spreading of "knowledge". This basic insight spurred the interest and discussions on the concept and different forms of knowledge. Knowledge became an object for knowledge generation, to put it one way. The focus of both researchers and practitioners was all of a sudden on the existence and value of the forms of knowledge that were not easily captured, controlled and spread, and yet very valuable to the performance and success of the organization. This actualized themes that earlier had only been of interest to specific research communities within organization theory, management. The field of AR arose partly from the recognition that the knowledge produced in conventional social research had so little practical use and impact on solving the organizational and societal problems it addressed. Therefore, to understand different forms of knowledge was at the core of AR discourse on the local and practical knowledge versus the production of general theories. Within OD, this divide between explication and analysis on the one hand and practical solutions and implementation on the other has been fundamental in constituting the field. The success of the book by Pfeffer and Sutton entitled *The Knowing-*

Doing Gap (1999), demonstrates clearly how important this problem is. What knowledge management contributed was to develop some new concepts, models, and theories to understand these different forms of knowledge.

The book that introduced the "soft" and practice-oriented approach in knowledge management was Nonaka and Takeuchi's *The Knowledge Creating Company* (1995). In addition to having a professional message that created interest, the book connected with the "zeitgeist," the general interest in understanding the Japanese competiveness. Every message emerging from Japan tended to have an attentive audience in the West, and the main perspective held by Nonaka and Takeuchi (op.cit.) in this particular book was that the West was excessively focused on explicit learning. In Japanese companies, there was more respect for the important role praxis-based and tacit knowledge plays in successful product development processes.

One model was the "SECI-model" where Nonaka and Takeuchi point out four basic processes of knowledge conversion. The first process is *socialization,* which is to disseminate tacit knowledge into new tacit knowledge for others. The second is *externalization,* which is to make tacit knowledge explicit and thereby available and meaningful for people other than oneself. The third process that they describe is the *combination* of available explicit knowledge, and the fourth process is what the authors call *internalization,* which is the transition where something known as good or right in theory is transformed into practice. The point is to identify and to conceptualize processes of developing and spreading knowledge by enhancing both explicit and tacit knowledge. In particular it was vital to emphasize how important tacit knowledge is to both innovation and efficiency.

The importance of the interaction between different forms of knowledge once again underscores the main argument of this book; that in order to develop an organization it is necessary to create opportunities for people to participate, to use their different forms of knowledge, to create new understanding and to convert the explicit learning into practices that work. To design and facilitate such arenas for learning is therefore essential to the understanding and practice of organizational change.

Arenas for Learning

A basic approach for creating learning in an organization is to form meeting places for social exchange (see the co-generative learning model in Chapter 4). Arena is defined as the social encounter in a material context that contributes to learning (Elden and Levin 1991). The essence behind the development of arenas is to establish dialogues between actors and to promote new frameworks for understanding. Furthermore, it is important to deliberately create arenas that open up possibilities to try things out in practice and to learn from new action patterns. These dialogues can create ideas, identify opportunities and contribute to decisions. Whether new collective behaviour is achieved depends on the existence of possibilities for practical training and reflection. Deliberate design of arenas is an important option for courses of action in leading change. The arenas create opportunities for dialogue and reflection grounded on shared praxis and experiences. The work forms that are described in Part II of this book can be considered input for a repertoire of such learning arenas.

What is Knowledge?

The traditional conception is that knowledge is a driving force for action. Implicit in this view is a distinction between reasoning (cognitive phenomena) and practical action. In Western culture, separation of mind and body can be traced back 300 years to the Enlightenment philosopher René Descartes. He gave intellectual capabilities precedence over manual skills. Gradually a conception arose that knowledge was mainly connected to how we think, and that manual work was disconnected from our intellectual capacity. Such a view of knowledge invites organizational thinking that separates performance and action from insight and knowledge about the practical work. This position underpins expert-driven organizational change and is ill-suited to create processes where participation and collective learning are viewed as the driving forces for development. It is necessary to develop an understanding of knowledge and action where performance of work and development of knowledge are integrated in the same process. The Cartesian split of mind and body gives little room for such a connection.

Learning from reading books takes solid precedence with respect to what is perceived as knowledge. We have learned to interpret texts as the actual expressions of insight and understanding. The explicit and analytic approach, where arguments and foundations create a chain that constitutes an explanation of phenomena, is what we have been taught. First we think, then we act, is a dichotomy that is intuitively appealing. It is after all the basis of Western education. This is how people have learned how to learn.

Explicit Knowledge (Knowledge Engraved in Texts)

There are alternative interpretations of what knowledge is. Firstly, we do not play down learning from texts. If so, writing this textbook on leading change would be paradoxical. The point is to position explicit knowledge as one of several possible conceptualizations of knowledge. Explicit knowledge primarily conveys factual knowledge. There is no reason to discuss the meaning of explicit factual knowledge. Factual knowledge represents an unassailable platform for knowledge-based action, but to restrict knowledge only to explicitly available knowledge is an overly limited approach.

The second important point of explicit knowledge is that texts and arguments exist independently of contexts. They live their own life independent of their creators. Getting access to insight that is conveyed through texts is up to the reader. Traditionally, the explicit form of knowledge has dominated the organization sciences. Early literature within OD was also characterized by the notion that explicit research-based knowledge was objective. The role of experts follows directly from this position. Scientific management, as Frederick Taylor presented it in his book of 1911, has influenced generations of researchers and practitioners in organizations. Taylor presented that work should be designed objectively by experts. This point of view is diametrically different from the ideas essential in co-generative learning. Taylor postulated that it is important to make a clear distinction between manual and intellectual work. Those working on the shopfloor should only be concerned with practical work, while planning and facilitation of existing work practices should be in the hands and heads of planners and engineers. In this perspective it fitted nicely with Descartes' Enlightenment perspective. Expert knowledge of work design (this is the knowledge in scientific management) was controlled by planners and engineers, while the experiences and insights of those who carried out the work had no value. Restructuring and development work was assigned to staff functions, and the managers had no intention of seeking knowledge from the ones who knew the everyday work. In scientific management it was seen as possible to develop "synthetic" knowledge of the basic elements in jobs, and then put these together in sequences for optimal work performance.

A position that holds that the participants' insights and competencies are essential factors for the design of an efficient organization is still considered a new trend. Designing organized work is very difficult if those concerned are not involved. The argument for including employees is based on the importance of motivating people for restructuring, and because employees hold knowledge that is necessary for restructuring an organization. Why is it that experts cannot acquire this knowledge?

Tacit Knowing (Knowledge in Operation)

The conception of knowledge as hidden can appear logically inconsistent. The story goes that during the doctoral dissertation defence of a researcher interested in tacit knowledge, the main opponent started as follows: "this dissertation should have remained unwritten because it deals with *tacit* knowledge". Of course it is possible to relate to tacit knowledge explicitly, even if the phenomenon is hidden. The ideas behind tacit knowing are ascribed to the Russian-American philosopher Michael Polanyi. He wrote a book in 1966 entitled *The Tacit Dimension*, in which the introductory argument is that we hold more knowledge than what we are able to verbalize. Polanyi uses two powerful arguments to substantiate the existence of the tacit dimension. First, he points out that we are able to recognize a person's face in a crowd of thousands of faces, but that we are not able to explain analytically why we recognize this particular face. Polanyi's second argument is children's acquisition of language. If it is the case that all our knowledge is preserved in words, a small child faces a formidable challenge in learning language. To master a language, we need grammatical and syntactic rules, but to understand rules, we need a language. A child without language cannot learn rules but is still able to acquire the language. Polanyi argues that individuals have knowledge that is an important part of our intellectual repertoire, without being able to verbalize this knowledge. This has been known as intuition, social intelligence, or gut feeling. We use these notions to acknowledge that we may see particular actions as right and sensible without being able to put it into words.

The concept of tacit knowledge has contributed an important dimension to the understanding of work. Performance of work has elements of knowledge that are not immediately accessible to the external observer. This knowledge is visible in what the individual is able to do, and not what the person can talk about. In other words, it is not possible to access this knowledge without participation from the one who possesses the skills. Consequently, it is impossible to develop change processes in organizations that are based on the employees (tacit) knowledge without participation from those people. Knowledge in organizations cannot be cultivated without participation and involvement from the employees that hold this knowledge as part of their daily work. Knowledge is described as something that is hidden, but at the same time has components that are explicit. An important point here is that people's interest in knowledge is closely related to daily work. This form of knowledge is practical knowledge.

Practical Knowledge (Knowing How)

The English philosopher Gilbert Ryle introduced this concept in 1949 in the book *The Concept of Mind*. In a discussion of forms of human understanding, Ryle developed the concepts *knowing that* and *knowing how*. It is the latter that is of interest in our further discussion. *Knowing that* largely overlaps with what we have previously identified as explicit knowledge. *Knowing how* roughly includes what we have called tacit knowledge. The basic idea is that humans are able to make their knowledge available to others through their actions. The knowledge behind these actions is described as practical knowledge. This is a fundamental form of knowledge, because in the widest sense it represents the foundation for human existence. It is through our actions that individuals are able to survive in society, and it is through concrete actions in an organization that members legitimize their position. Know how materializes in activity. This knowledge is woven into the individual's praxis. Practical knowledge does not exist independently of work, but through work. Polanyi uses Ryle's *knowing how* as a basis when he develops the tacit dimension. In the context of this book it is important to identify the tacit dimension through the individual's actions. In a study of craftsmanship, Thomas Tempte makes himself an advocate for vocational knowledge as "the practical intellect" (1991). The practical intellect is paralleled in conventional understanding of intellectual activity. They are just expressed in different ways.

Practical knowledge is essential to understand organizational change. Organizational change is an activity that contributes to tangible changes in the way employees work. The result of a development process should be measured by the organization's ability to work differently and hopefully better than before.

Consequently, change in practical knowledge is what one strives to refine so that new practices can emerge. It is important for the employees to develop new practical knowledge. Seen from the perspective of the co-generative learning model, construction of arenas for reflection and learning provides the basis for understanding practical knowledge, while also providing the foundation for development and change. In the next step, concrete experimentation with new work practices provides the basis for reflection and insight into the practical knowledge.

Reflection In and On Actions

Donald Schön (1983) argues for two dimensions in the reflection process. First, Schön states that it is possible to reflect in interaction with the action itself. He uses the relationship between a master and an apprentice as an example of such a reflection process. In cooperation with the master, the apprentice tries to understand the expert's knowledge practically through "conversing", both with the practical performance of a task and with the people who do the work. The second form of reflection is to reflect on what has been done. This is the form of reflection that will mainly take place in the arenas that are designed into an organizational change process, and which provides insight into previous actions. Reflection in action could be acquired by the participants in the OD process, if one is able to shape the change process so that, during the concrete change effort, one allows people with different expertise to work together on developing new solutions. It will then be possible to understand and learn practical knowledge.

6 Participation and Resistance to Change

Participation is not only the main approach to organizational change in this book. Participation also addresses the essence in modern organizing. Modern organizing might be seen as an attempt to engage members in collective efforts with as little resources as possible spent on coordination and control. The only way to achieve participation is through getting people truly involved. The same kind of argument is true for organizational change. We hold that the common experiences that change, develop or transform are so complex that they would be much better understood if change is conceptualized as a process of shaping collective learning processes in a participative approach, rather than as an analytical process.

In this chapter participation is primarily dealt with in a perspective of organizational change. This will be done based on presenting arguments that highlight participation from three different positions (Greenberg 1975). First, participation can be seen as a method to reduce alienation and increase opportunities for making work a source for development of our human capacities. Second, participation can be seen as a democratic right and an important value in work, just as it is a fundamental element of governance in a democratic society. Third, from a managerial point of view participation is a tool for making use of all relevant knowledge, while at the same time ensuring ownership of decisions and solutions.

We will also discuss how experiences of "resistance to change" can be understood through looking at them through the same perspectives. A common view is that resistance is best explained by conservative human nature, or as a result of actors pursuing narrow personal interests at the expense of what is best for the organization. The chapter will end with a reconceptualizing of resistance as normal and even a potentially positive capacity. The first effort in this chapter is to give a broad perspective on participation in organizational life.

A Humanistic Argument for Participation

The humanistic perspective on participation addresses the genuinely human side of work. It is obvious that working conditions impact employees' life situations both at work and in leisure time. This perspective is brilliantly formulated by Philip Herbst in his discussion of alternatives to hierarchical organizations, "the product of work is man" (Herbst 1977). Work organizations with high degrees of specialization and division of work may soon find that they have employees who are alienated by their work and prefer to act as cogs in a machine rather than as creative and knowledgeable workers.

As discussed in Chapter 1, one of the fundamental principles of classical organization theory is to shape a clear division between thought and action, between those who decide and those who perform work based upon the plans and decisions made by others. Frederick Taylor's (1911) argument was that the execution of work should not be a result of arbitrary subjective experiences, but derived from scientific analysis of work specified in detail how the work should be done. This principle defined the relationship between the leader and the subordinate, and between a team of expert planners and designers, with the workforce seen as only capable of performing manual work.

This distinction defined management and work organization in classical organization theory and also explain the lack of participation by subordinates in planning and execution of daily work. Participation modifies the fundamental distinction (Pateman 1970) between leaders and the ordinary employees. Similarly, motivation became an important theme in the work life of the 1930s precisely because the Tayloristic approach created jobs that were alienating and boring. It was no longer assumed that people would work because of their commitment to work or its outcome. There came a need for theories on what constituted good working conditions. In the Industrial Democracy Project in Norway that was presented in Chapter 3, participation was a fundamental value behind the search for new forms of organizing and improved job content. This was together with democratic values the main argument for participation. The programme addressed the industrial reality created by Tayloristic principles, and set the goal of reducing alienating work. The research team defined concrete principles regarding what each job should be aligned to in order to be a good job, and among these were opportunities to make decisions on at least a defined area related to one's own work situation.

Another example from the same tradition was efforts to find organizational solutions that made direct participation possible or necessary. The solution to this challenge was extensive use of "semi-autonomous work groups". The design principle of these groups was to create a clear boundary between the group and the rest of the organization where the group collectively had control over its own work. As long as the group could deliver the desired output and meet given efficiency standards, the members had the freedom to organize their internal work according to what they found appropriate. This "autonomy" was, as a principle for work organization, the direct opposite of extreme work control established in the Scientific Management approach decades earlier.

The Industrial Democracy Project pioneered participation, not only through principles of job design and team organization, but also by arguing for a more formal democratic approach to organizational change. An organization is a power structure where actors are holding different interest and power positions. A democratic principle would be that there should be a fair opportunity for everyone to argue their interests and to have a say in factors shaping daily life at work.

Participation as a Democratic Ideal

Another argument for participation is grounded in democratic values. People strive for a democratic society simply because it represents a preferable society to live in and be a part of. In the same way, democracy should also be an element of everyday work life. Accordingly, it is a legitimate argument that there is a fundamental right to influence one's own situation at work.

A fundamental feature of democracy is that solutions are achieved through interaction and negotiation, where involved parties accept the legitimacy behind other parties' demands and positions. On the one side, influence is exerted through direct participation in controlling one's own work.

On the other hand, indirect participation implies the election of representatives to negotiate and participate in decision-making on behalf of the constituency. Direct participation is not in itself controversial as an ideal, and approaches where people take more responsibility in their own jobs are welcomed by almost everyone. In representative democracy, elected representatives (often from unions) exert influence over the company's development through formal and informal procedures and processes. This is a practice with much more varied and controversial status in work life.

In some countries (US, UK and Australia as typical examples) employers will often consider unions as a threat to company development and profitability. The union, on the other hand, may look at the employer as a powerful actor who will sacrifice employee interests for short-term profit. In other countries, particularly in Scandinavia, this picture is very different. In these countries trade unions and managers to a greater extent see each other as legitimate parties. Unions negotiate their members' share of profits, but the parties spend much more time and interaction on extensive collaboration on company development, strategy development and value creation. In major parts of US industry it would most probably be unthinkable to invite unions as active partners in company development processes, while in similar parts of Scandinavian industry it would be unthinkable not to invite unions to participate.

One discussion on participation as democratic ideal is concerned with whether or not formal participation ensures real influence. In Scandinavia, two perspectives related to this issue have been debated in particular. The first is rooted in a discussion related to a change in national legislation in Norway to mandate that companies over a certain size should have a certain representation in company boards. This new legislation was a clear political intervention based on a democratic ideal designed to increase workers' influence. An interesting debate followed in the wake. Would the formal representation also mean real influence on the discussions and decisions in the board? The argument against was not about the overt power play, but how employee representatives might become the weaker part because of the significance of particular knowledge and "models".

Stein Bråten (1973) introduced the concept of "model monopoly" to describe this asymmetry of power. He argued that when actors discuss choices and decisions in a corporate board, the participants make sense of available information through different ways of reasoning. The models used to interpret a concrete situation are based on a person's experience and education. These "models" should be understood as encapsulating our understanding of particular relations between significant elements, for example, the elements that are relevant for judging a future investment, if a strategy is feasible, or if downsizing is necessary, and so on. If two parties exchange information and one masters all such models while the other does not, what consequences does this have for their joint decision-making process? The "model strong" actors can use any new information to make their own assessments and arguments stronger and clearer. The "model weak" actors will also be subject to new information, but are much less able to use this information to produce new arguments to support their interests. Bråtens point was that the employees' access to an arena such as the company's board does not necessarily make them more influential. Influence is not only about being represented on an arena for discussions and negotiation, but also on the knowledge and "model strength" of the participants.

Another theme in the discussion of real influence in participative processes is about "democratic dialogue" (Gustavsen and Engelstad 1986). This addresses the conditions in which dialogue on a participative arena can be assumed to be truly democratic. Will the strong hierarchical authority that may control daily operations also affect the participation in the company's development process? How is it possible to ensure that participating employees have real influence in such a mode that the strength of arguments and potential in new ideas are listened to without relating it to formal authority in the organization? One interesting approach to address this problem was not to address particular power relations per se, but rather to develop a set of rules for the process, that is, rules for a democratic dialogue (Gustavsen and Engelstad 1986). Following the rules would ensure that the process and dialogue would create real influence in the sense that it was the content of arguments and not formal or rhetorical power that impacted the actual decisions. For example, a rule could be that personal work experience is a valid basis for presenting an idea or argument. This type of thinking has particular significance when designing arenas for interaction between actors with different interests and power positions in the organization.

An important factor that emerges from formal democratic traditions of participation is that it also develops a collective competence in local problem-solving. There will always be conflicts of interest, particularly related to the change processes, and those conflicts are not in themselves a sign that something is wrong. What is important is how these controversies are handled prior to major problems for the organization and for future developmental work. In countries where there is a tradition of cooperation between the parties on the labour market and not only conflict-oriented negotiations, this tradition will also have shaped a mutual trust and arenas for cooperation that take care of the potentially more conflicting situations in processes of change.

Participation for Practical Problem-Solving and Mobilization of Competence

The third and last position we want to discuss is the one that has become the most obvious argument today, namely that participation is important because it creates better results. In Greenberg's (1975) article this was called the management position, primarily because the article saw profitability as primarily a management's field of interest. The profitability argument for participation can obviously take many forms. The first and perhaps most important is all about information and knowledge. The division of work that separates decision-making and planning from execution also means that there is an organizational division between those who through work experience have essential knowledge about the everyday challenges and opportunities, and those who formally make decisions about work and change. It is not difficult, theoretically or empirically, to argue that participation is important to ensure that decision-making is based on relevant and correct information.

An equally important and obvious point is the link between participation in the change process and the subsequent implementation process. An obvious challenge in traditional top-down change is the implementation of decisions and plans. There sometimes seems to be an underlying assumption that if the analysis is good and the decision is the right one, then implementation will be easy. As many will have experienced, this is very often not the case. Given that analysis and planning really is thorough, the main reason given is that the rest of the organization has not taken part in the learning process inherent in the analysis and development of solutions. An imperative favouring participation is that the actual implementation process is already starting with the process of understanding the challenges and creating solutions. A final key point is simply that those who have helped to shape the solutions will also find that they have ownership and therefore obligations to ensure that what they have developed will become reality. Those who have not participated in the first place do not experience this kind of ownership.

Resistance to Change

Asking experienced people in organizations what they think is the greatest challenge to the change process, "resistance to change" will certainly be the dominating answer. Just as clearly as this book argues for participatory processes of change, others will promote as their experiences and views that the most common problem is that members will not participate. "People do not want change" is a standard answer, referring obviously to other people and not to themselves. More or less the underlying argument is that "people are conservative and will react negatively to everything new". Fairly paradoxical is that almost everyone will have strong views that something really should be changed in their organization. It is probably easy to agree that people would rather be in charge of change than be the ones being changed. But how can a more systematic and fundamental discussion of resistance be launched? Why do so many see resistance to change as a reality and a challenge? Tentatively this question is addressed through some of the same angles discussed under the headlines of participation. The first main argument is that work creates people (even creates people who do not want change). The second perspective is that an organization is an arena for power, and some people resist potential solutions and ideas because they see them as contrary to their best interests. The third argument is that resistance may arise from a concern that suggested and decided changes are based on limited or faulty knowledge.

Acquired Passivity and Resistance

Is it basic human nature not to want change and is that why some people seem to be keen opponents to new initiatives and change processes? Is there, similarly, a group of people who are born with the desire to be told what to do and to otherwise be left in peace? The argument often heard is that many employees will not participate in the change process and will not accept change, no matter what it is about or how it is implemented. Apart from the fact that this is a sad perspective on human nature, we will also argue that it is a wrong and a devastating perspective.

Conceptualizing change as learning processes, it is important to understand how attitudes to one's own work and on change are results of hard learned experiences. Our basic position to leading change is that it is not just about creating solutions to specific challenges, but also to develop the organization's capacity and competence to deal with future development. Participatory-based change process creates resources in the organization in terms of a collective expertise that is developed and can be mobilized later. Similarly, detailed control systems and top-down implementation of change processes primarily teach people to be passive and to see themselves as disconnected with no personal responsibility for the company's further development.

Many individuals have never been expected to or had the opportunity to participate actively in development and change. The more alienating work is, the less likely are workers to have or experience control over the process and ownership of results, which again disengages them from participation in change activity. Our position is that where resistance to change (or indifference to change) is seen, it is not the result of basic human traits, but a consequence of learning from previous experiences in work and change processes. Furthermore, if the situation is such that some do not see it as meaningful to get involved or become involved in the change process, that alone is not a legitimate argument to let the organization be dominated by the same negative learning circles.

Resistance as Response to Conflict of Interest and Lack of Control

The argument for participation as a democratic right assumed that there would be conflicts of interest in any organization. Democracy in the workplace as well as in society in general is about being able to exert influence in the direction of one's own interests when there are differences. Participation is thus a way to be seen and heard and produces legitimacy of organizational solutions. Similarly, an obvious reason for resistance to change is that some people simply cannot find that the processes and solutions are compatible with their own interests, or they feel uncertain about whether or not their interests are heard. From a democratic perspective this is a legitimate basis for exercising resistance to a given change process. For example, there is every reason to expect people to be opponents to processes where they risk losing their job, salary, development opportunities and so on. In most cases, the process of change is not about such matters, but how can members know? This is a major cause of resistance to change because employees do not trust that they know or can influence all the changes. To use a metaphor, if the process of change is pictured as a row of carriages that should be moved in a certain direction, would attitudes be different if sitting in the rear carriage or in front and in control? It probably would. Would it make a difference if you trusted the driver? Of course. Would the experience of the journey be different if the curtains were down, or if the traveller were able to look out and see where in the landscape the row of carriages were heading? Certainly.

This metaphor presents clear arguments for participation, and it also presents one important reason why strong and competent trade unions may make the change process easier rather than more difficult, as they may produce legitimacy and a confidence among employees that their most basic interests are taken care of (including the basic interest that a competitive business makes jobs safer).

Resistance to Bad Solutions

We have already argued for a utility perspective as the most pervasive argument for participation in change processes. Participation in this perspective is important because it creates solutions that are both better and easier to implement. Similarly, we argue that an important source of resistance to change is that the change process is perceived to deal with the wrong challenges in the organization or generate unfortunate solutions. It may not be a correct conception from those who resist, but the point is that as a basis for resistance it should be recognized as legitimate and not categorized as a general conservatism. The organizational division between those who decide and plan the work and those who execute plans and decisions obviously creates a separation in access to information and knowledge. A gap is then built into the organization between an organizational layer with aggregated information and strategic goals and other parts with an experience-based understanding of practices, potential and of customer feedback. Resistance to some planned change from parts of the organization should then not be surprising, and participation may simply become the practical approach to bridging the organizational gap.

Participation as Fundamental for Organization and Change

Organizing is a collective effort and organizational change implies that members of the organization to work differently. The implication is that some kind of participative approach will be needed for any change effort to succeed. Most organizations simply search for ways to get people involved, and some leaders find this to be very difficult as it creates a sense of losing control. In the next chapter, we will address in particular the leadership challenges in organizational change processes.

7 Leading Participatory Change

Theories of what constitutes good leadership often centre the attention on the personalities and personal traits of a leader. Skill, traits, attitudes, and behavioural patterns are the main factors that describe the leader and explain their (presumed) success. It is not difficult to understand why there is so much focus on the personal characteristics of the leader. The influence from the mechanistic understanding of organizations still dominates how leadership is conceptualized and understood. This Tayloristic or Weberian account of an organization outlines it as a carefully-designed machine to produce a given result, where both people and technology are pieces of this machine. Given this framework, the leader plays a role as the mastermind who, together with a staff of experts, keeps the machine running smoothly. This basic perception defined the knowledge base of leadership shaped by personal traits and capacities. Essential variables in leadership would accordingly be capacities like intelligence, self-confidence, determination, integrity and sociability, as well as technological, human and conceptual skills and finally operating style (Northouse 2004).

Today there is a (near) consensus that this individualistic understanding of leadership is no longer entirely satisfying. The break with the image of organizations as hierarchically controlled machines leads to a search for alternative answers to what constitutes good leadership. If the relevant knowledge is no longer assumed to be centralized at the top of a controlling hierarchy, but instead distributed in the organization, what are the implications for good leadership? If the ideal is not the stable but the constantly changing organization, how does that change our understanding of leadership? If production is geographically distributed and the organization has a high alert on creating ideas and knowledge, what difference will this make on how we conceptualize and recognize good leadership?

These kinds of questions and discussions have expanded the field of leadership theory into a cacophony of conceptualizations, self-help tips and seductive success stories that all seek to reveal what this "new" form of leadership is about. We will, however, not take on the task of reviewing and assessing the alternative positions. Rather, the point of departure is constituted two main lines of reasoning in the broad discourse on what constitutes good leadership, and we will contribute to one of these.

The first main direction is a continuation of what is described as the heritage from classical organizational theories, where the leaders are some kind of super-humans who have the capacity to make extraordinary things happen through their inherent qualities. The aim for research on leadership is accordingly to reveal these qualities. One such contemporary and very popular theory is transformational leadership, which is an idealized leadership model that has been very influential over the last decade and that is still given more attention. Transformational leadership rose from studies of "great men" who have led nations, popular movements or organizations and who have been successful in creating large scale changes either for the good or bad. Transformative leadership theory aims at explaining why these and similar leaders seem to be able to lead through large and challenging change processes, mostly with high levels of support from employees (or citizens or members). Bass (1990) defines this leadership approach through some specific ways in which the leader influences:

- Idealized influence. Underlines that the leader influences by showing a kind of behaviour that can be a model for others. The authority of the unquestioned ideal shown by the leader's public performance.

- Inspiring motivation. Emphasizes the leader's ability to formulate visions and ambitions which co-workers can recognize, and which they can take part in and make their own.

- Intellectual stimulation. The leader holds as a basic assumption about co-workers that they want challenges, desire renewal and are ready to take responsibility.

- Individualized attention. The ability to "see" individual co-workers and the unique potential that each person has.

In some ways this is a renaissance of the charismatic leader, where organizational performance and particular results are explained by personal characteristics and a leader's somehow magical ability to create followers behind themself. The danger is that one may end up advocating leadership approaches where critical and constructive voices are silenced and the only thing that matters is to become a true follower. Further, there is hardly any research that underpins the operational effect of transformational leadership.

Another example of a popular contribution in defining the great leader is the "Level 5 Leadership" identified by Jim Collins in *From Good to Great*. He found that characteristics of the leaders who were at the top of the great companies were not observable among the leaders of the companies that performed above average. In the great companies Collins found almost shy and humble leaders who were at the same time brutally honest and with a strong will. He found leaders who were taking responsibility for poor results themselves while giving others credit for what went well. In the study Collins didn't look particularly for leadership theories to explain the differences between the groups of companies, but he found the evidence to be clear. The leaders were different in these groups of companies.

An elaborate criticism of these theories about ideal super-human leaders is not intended here, other than stating that the theories do not give much advice to the leader facing a need to do something to change and develop the organization.

Attention is on the contrary directed to a different line of research on and discussions about leadership, where the aim is to understand leadership as a practice shaped in the interaction between leaders and members, in the concrete sociotechnical operation, and related to the actual market conditions. The interesting question is not who the leader is, but on how leadership is performed and how it is a practice that is embedded in the everyday work of the organization. It is this practice that creates the factual results. How does the leader engage with the organization in order to create change and desired results? This is the grounding perspective for our conceptualization of leadership.

The interest is specifically related to leadership of development and change processes. We emphasize that it is the organization's collective ability to generate results, including the creation of desired change, that is important. The legitimacy of leaders and leadership is because it is supposed to create results. It has no justification in itself. It is only through the organization's performance, be it financial results, quality results, contributions to society or employee development or any other defined measures, that leadership can claim a value. In this perspective the personality of the leader is only interesting through praxis unless it is presented in a particular organizational context where the leader's personality contributes in a particular way.

The point of departure is that leading organizational change deals with encouraging and enabling the organization to meet identified challenges and to develop its capacity to meet future challenges. Our theoretical position is a conceptual understanding of the organization as a product of previous collective learning processes. It is the shared learning from those processes that has created the current organization. The construction of an organization is, in other words, a consequence of how the learning has unfolded over time. The essence of leadership, given this perspective, is to lead the learning processes. This is a dramatic shift from viewing leadership as personal skills or traits because leadership has turned to be a question of how to facilitate learning processes. Given this line of reasoning, it becomes obvious that the leader cannot settle on what should be the concrete outcome for everyone participating in the learning processes. The leader should be in charge of what kind of learning processes are needed and also be active in facilitating these learning opportunities.

Furthermore, leadership as leading learning processes is important for developmental and long-term resource building in an organization. This developmental work is engraved in daily operation of the organization. Every day, products and services have to be produced. The coordination and control over daily operation is also an essential issue in leadership, but that is not the theme for this book. It is not left out because it is unimportant, but because the focus is on development and building competency.

Returning to the previous argument, leading change deals with the ability to involve people, challenge theories of action and facilitate learning processes in the organization. This is outlined in our general model in Chapter 4.

Given the model of learning and the understanding of organizational change leadership as a starting point, what will be the particular roles and responsibilities associated with leading participatory processes of organizational change? In this form of leadership the following elements are essential:

a. clarifying the boundary conditions within which the change processes operate;

b. shaping of positive communicative and learning conditions where one's own and others' basic assumptions may be challenged and inquired about;

c. designing and facilitating arenas for learning, based on an understanding of alternative work forms, principles of participation and conditions for learning;

d. institutionalizing mechanisms that increase the organization's capacity for handling future needs for change.

i. Leading Participatory Change Involves Setting and Explicating Boundary Conditions, Structural Changes and Guiding Principles

Participatory change starts with a collective approach to creating a shared understanding of what kind of problem or challenge confronts the organization and what potential difficulties and possibilities for the change process could be seen on the horizon. It is important to create a realistic picture of the space of possibilities and name limitations and borders. All change will take place within certain conditions determined by the sociotechnical conditions and by the political economy. A good and solid change process demands that these conditions are made explicit and clear to everyone involved. To lead participatory change processes therefore involves clarifying what these conditions are and the legitimacy of these conditions. A participatory approach to strategy processes will typically involve a wide range of possible discussions and change initiatives that open up perspectives that were not reflected when the change activity started. Often there are clear boundaries for the change processes that have not been communicated or understood by the people involved in the change process. An overall strategy may be identified and agreed upon, and the participatory process implies the organization in developing ways to make the strategy happen. If a crisis may be seen in the horizon which would shape a boundary condition that no-one can choose to ignore. Then the change process will focus the attention on finding solutions and ways to meet the observed crisis.

Distancing ourselves from the approaches that see organizing as principally about designing and redesigning structures, we acknowledge that it is important to recognize and understand how structural decisions influence everyday work as well as possibilities for change. All organized activity involves limiting some actions and opening up to other types of activity. Design of structures is to create connections and divisions, create organizational units, assign responsibility, allocate resources, and so on. Developmental processes may identify needs for changing such structural conditions, but making formal decisions is clearly a leadership task. Creating the new organization of work and realizing the potential for improvement is, however, a collective effort.

Leading participatory change involves allocating resources for development and defining and making explicit some clear and fundamental principles for the leader, the participants and for the collective processes that will guide the change activity. Who will decide what? Will critical voices be heard? How can people find time to engage in change processes and at the same time take care of daily operation? Are there any guarantees with respect to future conditions of employment? There is no point in inviting participation in change processes where the outcome has already been decided on. It is not possible to involve people unless daily work allows for involvement in change activity.

ii. Leadership is to Facilitate Dialogues that Enable Collective Learning

In Chapters 4 and 5, we have emphasized organizational change as a learning process and dialogue and collective reflection as essential parts of learning processes. An important element of leading participatory change is therefore to create the climate and facilitate dialogues that make such learning processes possible. A meeting or a confrontation in a hostile environment where people are essentially defensive and mistrust each other is obviously not productive in a development process. Leading participatory change is to invite others to engage in dialogues that potentially challenge current theories of action, and to test one's own and others' ideas so that they can be challenged and possibly improved. The underlying theoretical framework is elaborated in Chapter 5.

The normal situation in an organization is not and should not be that members are constantly questioning if the right things are being done in the right way. Most of what is done in a normal work situation is straightforward and routine, which of course is a prerequisite for efficient operation. At the same time, learning and development is about starting processes to challenge and improve the prevailing reasoning and praxis. Sometimes there will be an obvious need to do things differently, but often signs will be ambiguous, or new ambitions or assessments will arise, so that the need for change becomes questionable. Thus, raising the right challenges at the right time is a basic leadership challenge. To be able to lead such processes is therefore obviously means to have not only substantive leadership knowledge and process skills, but also substantial knowledge about technology, work processes, products, customers and market. In other words, knowledge that will be essential for facilitating such learning processes.

iii. Leading Participatory Change Implies Understanding and Designing/using Different Arenas for Learning

A basic precondition for leadership of change processes is to create arenas for learning and change. Organizations already have some formal or informal (potential) learning arenas that are set up to support everyday work, cooperation, problem solving, or the need to formalize some decision-making. To create learning arenas should not be understood simply as adding new meetings to already busy working days, but to recognize that existing meetings and arenas can be transformed into efficient tools and drivers of organizational change process. The implication is that existing leadership meetings or current running strategy processes have to be designed to facilitate broad learning processes. Another possibility is to substitute conventional training courses with different learning opportunities. Another option is to shape meeting spaces where collective reflection is possible. A miniature arena in this respect is for example space that allows people to talk in front of the coffee machine. It should also be obvious that the introduction of new technology should give room for learning and developmental processes (Levin 1998).

The most important leadership principle that should guide the design and use of arenas for learning is that is to encourage employees to become engaged and involved, take ownership and responsibility and use their knowledge and energy to change their own practice because they have to be involved. To design arenas for learning is therefore to understand who can and should participate, and then to design the opportunities to make it possible to truly participate and engage in change. No simple recipes are at hand. There are just different answers to the same obvious questions; Who should be involved and how can it be made to happen?

iv. Leadership of Organizational Change Involves Increasing the Organization's Capacity to Change

Leading change is not concerned with solving the immediate challenges at hand. There will always be new problems and new opportunities and therefore always a need for initiating new change processes. Therefore to develop future capacity for change is an essential leadership challenge. When "the learning organization" was conceptualized by Peter Senge and colleagues in the 1990s, it was framed as a matter of developing a set of disciplines when addressing the individual and the collective. These disciplines would make individuals and groups capable of recognizing, analysing and giving appropriate response to needs for change. Collective visions should be shaped, team skills created, personal capacities enhanced, communicative skills improved, and finally a good understanding of how activities are interlinked in time and space in a dynamic whole should be developed.

In a participative approach to organizational change, some aspects will be particularly important. First, leading participatory change is a process that in itself has to be learned. To facilitate discussions with actors with different interests without losing sight of the overall aim and direction is in itself a skill. To work in development projects and teams, see opportunities, create common ground and structure collective work processes involves some other forms of skills. To develop participatory change as a kind of institutionalized practice is not just about developing relevant leadership skills. It is just as much about developing collective practices, practices that can only be mobilized and developed through collective local action. This is not just about creating process knowledge but also about having a power balance between legitimate interests. This point was well illustrated by Finn Borum (1980) in his description and analysis of a development process at a hospital department. The change processes involved both doctors and nurses, and Borum's point was that the two groups had different interests and very different skills and power positions when it came to influencing the process and solutions. The doctors had well-developed skills and experience in promoting their interests, while the nurses lacked these strategic skills. Thus, developing this skill was a precondition for the nurses to be able to take part without the risk that their interests would be trampled on.

Second, a very important element in change processes is trust. Clarifying boundary conditions and fundamental principles is important to reduce the uncertainty and potential resistance associated with the uncertainty. However, the only way to create a fundamental trust in such principles is through shared experiences that let participants experience that participative principles and promises are real.

In Scandinavian countries in particular, the extensive union and employer cooperation has been essential in developing and institutionalizing local (formal) participatory practices that are not only mobilized when there is conflict, but also in OD processes. In fact, while formal arrangements have their origins as instruments for negotiation, most time is spent on cooperation about development and change.

Leading Change Processes – Art or Profession?

The view that knowledge of leadership can be developed through research has always had a counterpart in a view of leadership as being something in between art and craft. Leadership as praxis is, after all, as old as social organization. A claim is that it is best learnt in the same way as other practical professions, where skills are developed through supervised or mentored experience-based learning.

Moreover, strong criticism of leadership as research-based praxis has come from Henry Mintzberg (2004), who is a central researcher of leadership. In particular, he has fought the trend that people who receive an MBA at a business school are only trained to manage the intellectual side of theories of leadership and not in the practice of management. It is not difficult to join this criticism, and one of the explanations for this development is that behaviourist and objectivist positions lead people to think that humans and organizations function according to laws that research uncovers and provides as tools for the leader.

Viewing the organizational reality as a continuous and dynamic formation process within opportunities and frames, the leader is necessarily also modelled more as a participant in these processes than as a designer and controller of the actions of others. At the same time, professional perspectives on leadership play an important part in development of leadership praxis. Donald Schön (1983) contributed with an important understanding of how professionals learn through daily practice. He introduced the concepts of reflection in action and reflection on action. The latter is understood as a process of extracting learning after the activity has been performed.

Learning and praxis should not be strictly sequential activities, in which learning creates a foundation for subsequent passive execution of praxis. Reflection in action indicates the ability to learn (reflect) directly from on-going activity. Reflection in and on actions is a cornerstone for development of leadership practice whether it is a novice working with experienced leaders or is in the process of securing continued learning and development for the leader.

Reflection without concepts and positions that challenge the individual's mental understanding and practical skills shapes meagre learning opportunities for the practitioner. Our position is to view research based theory on leadership as a "discussion partner" in reflection on praxis, and the concepts of the field as something that experimentally are used to fashion a language for reflection. In other words, the leadership field and leadership praxis produce the best contributions to development when they are closely intertwined.

PART II
WORK FORMS IN LEADING PARTICIPATIVE CHANGE

Part I of the book has presented a conceptualization of organizational transformation as a participative change process built on the co-generative learning model. This model is built on the assumption that learning dialogues enhance mutual learning. The important issue for leading change processes is to construct appropriate arenas for learning. In this perspective an arena consists of both the involved actors and the material structure within which learning is expected to take place. In leading change it is critical to choose good and relevant arenas for communication and learning. This selection implies decisions on which communication processes create good learning opportunities, who should participate and how these processes should be located in time and space. Making these decisions results in the application of an appropriate work form. A major argument is that a competent leader of change is skilful in choosing appropriate work forms, given the actual problem situation and in the concrete material and social context.

A number of different work forms are available. They can be picked from the repertoire of group dynamic processes, from researcher and, last but not least, from the literature on OD. An important part of being a leader of organizational change is therefore to be able to understand the nature of the problems or challenges at hand, to be familiar with alternative sets of methods or work forms and to have the necessary skills to use and facilitate them.

This may seem very basic, but practice shows that most leaders or even consultants in change management have a very limited repertoire, which makes it very easy to choose the same approach regardless of the situation at hand. In our view, it is imperative that the design of the change process is based on the specific challenges, what parts of the organization are or should be involved and the available time and resources. In other words, the core of the leader's competence is to be able to interpret the situation, understand the nature of the change process that is needed and choose an appropriate design of a change process. The choice of methods and work form depends on what type of learning arenas are deemed appropriate in the given situation. Finally, selecting appropriate work form has to be done in cooperation with problem owners.

In Part II of the book we have made a broad selection of work forms that, in our experience, have shown great potential to create good and sustainable learning processes.

In Chapter 8, Levin introduces how leaders and change agents can perform an initial organizational analysis that combines using a sound theoretical approach with a practical participative approach. The work form is in part based on a grounded theory approach to establish knowledge about social phenomena, and the possible use of metaphors and multi-framework perspectives in organization theory. The organizational analysis is a basis for being able to make a good initial design of a participative development process. In Chapter 9, Levin presents search conferences as a model for designing conferences that are based on a high degree of participation both in deciding on what problems to tackle and how to plan for participative development strategies. The search conference builds on mutual planning and ends with participants engaging in concrete work to solve pertinent problems. In Chapter 10, Senese present her use of World Café as a very open and inviting work form in which rather complex problems can be addressed in such a way that a large number of members of an organization or community can take part in the overall collective learning. In Chapter 11, Martin address situations where there are conflicting interests, and shows and discusses how there conflicts can be resolved using negotiation-procedures and strategies- Finally, in Chapter 12, Røyrvik present an approach for using Learning Histories to facilitate learning from important situations and processes, and where the different voices, experiences and positions are put in the forefront and established as important input to further collective learning.

The work forms that are presented in the following chapters are only a small selection of available instruments. The intention is to create an introduction to the potential for learning and development given the presented work forms which also will give a rough perspective of the diversity of possible ways of engaging in OD.

8 Organization Analysis

Before initiating change processes in an organization, it is necessary to establish an understanding of how the particular organizational unit is organized and managed. This challenge is equally important for the problem owners (members of the organization) as for the outsider (consultant, leader) who will be in charge of the development process. In a perspective of the co-generative model of OD, the argument is that OD can only be carried out professionally if the participants have established an understanding of how the particular organization operates. The process of creating this insight of an organization's structure and processes is what we define as an organization analysis.

Far too often, it becomes evident that OD consultants sell a solution before they form a professionally founded opinion of what characterizes the actual organization. It is easy to see how large international consulting firms profile their products according to current trends in management literature and often sell a solution before they have asked what the organization's problem is. To have the skills to carry out an organizational analysis is an incontestable and fundamental professional requirement for those who are responsible for change processes.

There are several important arguments for carrying out an organization analysis. First, it is essential that the person who will be responsible for a change process has a professionally based understanding of the particular organization. The emphasis is on *professionally based* analysis because it is far too easy that a few scattered impressions would colour the understanding of the organization. We argue strongly against this. It is a fundamental requirement of professionalism that those who are responsible for the process in co-generated learning develop an independent, well-founded and reasoned perspective of the organization in question. In the same way, it is important that the local problem owners also develop insight on how the organization operates. In change management it is further decisively important to create a process in which those who are involved locally can take part in the knowledge development, creating an understanding of the particular organization. The aim of such a process is to establish a mutual understanding of specific aspects of the organization, while each team or department also establishes their own perspective with regard to insight into their own reality. The challenge in change management is to form a process in which shared insight is co-generated, while also leaving space for the stakeholders' interests to be a source for interpretation and understanding of their own situation.

What is an Organization Analysis?

In short, an organization analysis involves a systematic effort to establish insight into the characteristics of an organization. This kind of insight is in no way reserved for management or OD experts. Local stakeholders need also to develop knowledge and understanding of their own organization. This is a natural part of daily life, and in this respect it is an important part of the organization's knowledge platform. Initially, the organization analysis can be limited to the leader or the outsider's systematic effort to understand the organization's routines and knowledge base. Moreover, an analysis can contribute alternative frames of reference, which in turn can then create other interpretations than the local ones. In this way, the analysis establishes new perspectives, which in turn can create new and potentially fruitful ways of understanding an organization's operational activity and knowledge system. A third perspective on organization analysis is to view it as a learning process which involves both local stakeholders and external experts. In this view, the analysis is a co-generative learning process in which local insight is coupled with external expertise to potentially create new and fruitful understanding.

It is important to emphasize that a professional academic standard is assigned to the organization analysis, which makes it something more than the experiential knowledge system held by the employees. The organization analysis, as it is treated in this book, is based on the use of research-based methodology and knowledge of organization and management. With regard to this, we emphasize that theories on organization and management are neither unambiguous nor independent from the context in which they are used. This was discussed in Chapters 1 and 2. A wide range of theories and analytical frameworks is available, which is a strength, because it allows the participants to choose fruitful explanatory frameworks from the diversity of models and interpretations in organization theory.

In principle, an organization analysis can be structured on the basis of prevailing theories in organization and management. Further, there will be many competing theories existing alongside each other. Depending on the perspective that is chosen, different aspects of the organization will seem important. In other words, the selected point of departure will decide what is seen. In many ways this may seem like a fundamental weakness of the field, as there is no agreed upon position to what is a good theory. It is not incidental therefore, that *fruitful* is preferred as the criterion for judging the applicability of a theoretical construct guiding the organization analysis. The important question is not whether a theory in itself is true, but whether it improves our insight into organizations. The fruitfulness of a theory is influenced by what the goal of the analysis is and what characterizes the particular situation and the people who make up the organization.

Thus, the professional platform of the organization analysis is shaped by the theoretical perspectives that govern the analysis. In many respects, there is significant power in selecting points of view that were not previously present in an organization. "Foreign" theories have an innovative potential in situations where local truths have been established over a long time. A further strength of the academic perspectives is that scientific theories often have high internal consistency, in the sense that they build on research. For example, by applying a particular theory the participants will be able to perceive relationships that were not clearly visible before. Another strength of the organization analysis is that it is based on a well-defined methodological foundation. In this respect, knowledge which is developed through methodological rigour will contribute to insights that build on the strength of the scientific method. Knowledge which is developed on the basis of a rigorous apparatus of methodology will often create interesting contrasts to the local frameworks of understanding, and it is unnecessary to discuss whether research-based insight is better than local understanding. What is important is whether any contrasts contribute to a development of new insight, both for the members of the organization and for the outsiders. The methodological approach for which we argue follows a handful of qualitative techniques as outlined in "Grounded Theory" (see, among others, Glaser and Strauss 1967; Corbin and Strauss 2008; Charmaz 2006).

Methodological Approach of the Organization Analysis

The arguments used in the previous paragraphs may easily create an illusion of a deductive positivistic organization analysis dominated by theory. This is not at all the intention. Our position is that research-based understanding of organizations creates a platform from which one can view the organizational landscape. The interpretation of this terrain is based on the models and theories that form the participants' intellectual ballast, but one will not know how matters actually are until being confronted with the domain of the organizations.

Furthermore, this image can be translated into concrete and specific interpretations through the application of a stringent methodology. The underlying ideas in this methodological angle of attack are "grounded" on Grounded Theory. In brief, a mapping of the organizational territory using Grounded Theory forwards demands on two levels:

1. The willingness and ability by the involved to listen systematically to people's opinions of their own work situation, in such a way that it enables understanding of the organization from the employees' point of view.

2. A solid theoretical platform built on organization theory, which is an essential tool because this is an analytical framework that helps systematize the understanding of an organization.

The point of departure for the organization analysis must be an ability to listen to all members of the organization. The insight which is created in these conversations will then be systematized in a creative balance between concrete analysis of data from the conversations and alternative interpretations given by different theoretical positions. This is an analytical strategy which is mainly inspired by Grounded Theory. The initial task is to construct an understanding of the organization based on data collected from conversations and interviews. These data are then subjected to a systematic and structured analysis. The next step is to map these data onto different theoretical positions. This couples creative and flexible interpretation with a systematic Grounded Theory approach.

Step 1: Listen to Members of the Organization

The first step of the organization analysis is to "go to the source," that is, to interview and talk to people on all levels. A few simple questions can form a point of departure:

What does your work consist of?

What challenges do you have in your work?

What problems do you have in your work?

What is a good job?

These questions are a good for establishing a conversation that will provide insight into the life and activities of the organization. These conversations are recorded in minutes or transcriptions of the conversations, which now constitute the data that form the basis for the first analysis. Often, one will begin by interviewing a small number of people, and then look at how these stories can be interpreted. The coding method in Grounded Theory is very helpful in this analysis. The coding involves taking all the statements from the interviews and conversations and giving a code to each statement. If, for example, there are statements like *"I can't do this because it will provoke other people in the department. We don't agree on how the work should be done,"* is coded as conflict (first sentence) and job ambiguity (second sentence). The entire material is coded and then it is organized in larger categories, which gradually structure the material. This texture then provides an insight into what seem to be the important features of the organization. By this means, the external change agent or leader are ready for the next step, which is to interpret this insight in the light of theories and research in the field.

Step 2: Creative and Constructive Analysis

In this step, the external change agent seeks to link research-based knowledge of the field with the concrete data and analysis gained through interviews and conversations. Theories and research-based statements help create a structure that binds categories together into possible models of explanation. *Possible* is an important word here, because at this level one only has a glimpse of the contours of some relationships and problems that have to be explored further. First, one has to gather additional data by talking to more employees, and at this level it is natural to ask more specific questions. Second, it is natural to look for alternative models of explanation. It is pointed out in the Introduction to this book that there is no single theoretical position that can explain all phenomena in an organization. Therefore, it is necessary for the outsider to show theoretical flexibility. This will in turn open up new perspectives which make it necessary to go back and ask new and more precise questions. This initial step has provided a certain insight into the organization's life and activities. This can be returned to the organization in such a way that locals can give feedback on our interpretations and assumptions.

Step 3: Involving Employees in the Analysis

The initial organization analysis can and should be communicated back to the problem owners in the organization. This will be an important step in establishing co-generated learning between stakeholders in the organization and the outsider who is responsible for the development process. By establishing this feedback process, we also create a basis for quality control of the analysis. If the employees indicate that they are on familiar terms with the analysis, it is clear that important features of the organization have been identified. On the other hand, if the employees give no signal of recognition, it is important to carry out a thorough discussion in which one shows from which data the conclusions have been drawn. This will be an important way of involving employees, which can in turn provide a basis for mutual interpretation and new insight for both parties.

The importance of this step cannot be overstated. It represents a fundamental condition for a participatory development process. If employees are not given the opportunity to create an understanding of their own organization, participation will easily become an illusion. A condition for genuine participation is that those concerned have a knowledge platform which is based on their own interests, and this may, in the type of feedback process that we recommend, make important contributions to the problem owners' development of an independent perspective.

We imagine that steps 1, 2 and 3 will run for as long as is necessary to ensure that the OD person has sufficient insight to take responsibility for staging a development process. Likewise, it is important to ensure that the organization analysis runs long enough for the problem owners also to establish a sufficiently solid foundation of insight into their own organization.

Use of Conceptual Platforms

So far the theoretical backdrop for the organization analysis has been treated as if it were fairly unambiguous. A traditional understanding of theoretical platforms is that they are intellectual constructs that are intended to interpret experiences forming a potentially consistent image. Within a scientific position of positivism, theories predict outcomes and events. Within hermeneutics, theories provide explanatory force, while theories within AR tend to provide insights for finding and selecting practical solutions for relevant problems. In the OD perspective, the requirement for theoretical construction is to map experiences from a perceived reality in order to create a system of social, economic and technological relationships that are as consistent as possible. These theoretical constructions subsequently provide a basis for deriving arguments for the choice of variables to include in the analysis.

In their book *Reframing Organizations,* Bolman and Deal (1984) create a research-based understanding of organization and management, formulated in four different frames: structural, human resource, political and symbolic. A structural frame sheds light on formalized social and technological structures. A human resource frame emphasizes the description of human life in organizations. A political frame provides understanding of political processes and power relationships in organizations, while a symbolic frame helps create an understanding of the realities created by people and culture in organizations. An important point for Bolman and Deal (1984) is that by using these frames makes it possible to discover aspects of organizations that have not previously been visible. They call this "reframing". A new frame can give stakeholders an understanding that provides them with entirely new options for further action. The ideas on which Bolman and Deal based their structuring of organization theory can be found in what we have already described in the creative application of reframing. Furthermore, the frameworks are fruitful because they enable us to see the complexity of an organization, as different positions show us different sides of the organization.

Gareth Morgan builds another foundation for analysing organizations. In the book *Images of Organization* (1986) he introduces metaphors as the key to understanding organizations. Morgan defines a metaphor as:

> *For the use of metaphor implies a way of thinking and a way of seeing that pervade how we understand our world generally ... the metaphor frames our understanding of the man in a distinctive yet partial way. (1986: 12–13)*

One of the interesting aspects of a metaphor is that it always produces a one-dimensional understanding. As some interpretations are emphasized, others tend to fade into the background. In other words, a metaphor gives an overarching insight into a new phenomenon, as the image from the metaphor is used to focus our attention. For example, a person can be characterized an old salt, automatically creating an interpretation of the salty sailor who has weathered more than a few storms in his life.

Morgan presents eight metaphors in his book. The first is based on an image of organizations as machines, dominated by strict and tight structures. The contrast to this understanding is a metaphor which portrays organizations as biological organisms where growth, learning and development are central features. What Morgan calls the brain-metaphor directs our attention to an understanding of self-organizing and self-controlled units. The fourth metaphor depicts organizations as cultural systems, and emphasis is on showing how people create the social reality that is an organization. The political metaphor depicts organizations as arenas in which power and conflict decide access to and use of the organization's resources. A rather negative metaphor presents organizations as mental prisons, where psychological forces inhibit the actors' development. The seventh metaphor constructs insight in organizations that are changing and developing. The eighth metaphor is a view of organizations as instruments of domination and control.

Morgan's frames have a different basis than those of Bolman and Deal. Their frames are strictly analytical in the sense that they represent unified theoretical constructs (Bolman and Deal 1991). Their strength is their analytical stringency. Morgan's metaphors are generative in that the metaphorical

147

portrayal forms a basis for creative and intuitive understanding of organizations (Morgan 1986). Portrayals enable us to see relationships and connections by transferring an image from an experiential world to map an organizational reality. Recognition and transference of intuitive understanding to holistic represents the metaphors' creative strength.

Often frames and metaphors are confusingly mixed. The metaphorical depictions of organizations are, of course, based on academic concepts and theories, but they are adapted in the metaphor's "pictorial" logic, while the frames are joined together in a theoretical platform.

Conclusion

Carrying out an organization analysis before starting an OD process is important for two reasons. First, through the organization analysis, the outsider establishes a professionally well-founded understanding of the organization in question. Second, the analysis will contribute to a co-generated understanding of what the core problems and challenges are in the organization. In this chapter, we have argued that a variant of Grounded Theory is a useful tool in an organization analysis in which a coupling between systematic qualitative analysis and constructive and creative use of different theoretical frameworks and metaphors will provide the necessary insight and understanding of the organization in question.

9 Search Conferences

Search conferences are a much-used work form that shape arenas for participative planning and development. The theoretical model behind a search conference is a participative process aimed at combining a description of a problem area with the development of a vision for a desirable future. In addition, a search conference also generates diverse strategies and actions aiming at reaching desired goals, collectively prioritizing the best strategies, and forming plans for implementation. In short, search conferences help develop understanding of a problem, prioritize what is important and ensure that someone starts working actively to reach the desired solutions.

Participants in a search conference alternate between work in groups and presentations and discussions in plenary. They work with peers (like-minded people) and have to learn to cooperate in groups with a cross-section of the stakeholders that are represented in the conference. Many find that running a search conference works as talent scouting, because the criteria for participation are different from those commonly used by companies or communities. As a new and unusual arena, a search conference allows new actors to present themselves.

The search conference is a method which has its origins in AR, and research groups in Norway and Australia have dominated its development. The first search conference in Norway was carried out in a fishing community and was aimed at developing strategies for development of business and social life in this active coastal community (Engelstad and Haugen 1979). The main actor in the development of search conferences on the Australian continent has been Merrelyn Emery (1999). In Australia, the research group around Emery has been highly active in marketing the "art" of running search conferences. Workshops have been held on almost every continent. The Australian tradition has had an aspect of dogmatism, where its followers have preached that there is only one correct form. We do not support this point of view. Following the underlying mindset in this book, our opinion is that it is the assessment of the local specific challenges that must set the guidelines for the design of the particular learning arenas.

Our experience is that search conferences are an unusually robust method. There are several examples of organizational blunders not having harmful effects on the process of the conference. There is reason to believe that participants' motivation and commitment when working with their own problems are the main guarantees of a positive result.

The Overarching Structure

A search conference may ideally last for two days. Two sets of factors are important in this regard. First, a two-day conference allows participants to establish relationships, because they will then, among other things, have dinner together and will often be staying in the same place. When a search conference is held in a place where participants can stay the night, it has the benefit that participants are removed from their daily tasks. This allows them to focus all their attention on the conference. The evening and night also give participants time to reflect and learn from the challenges and learning that the first day has contributed. A smart routine is to start the next day by asking whether anyone has pondered on anything or has any new ideas since the previous day. This will often give rise to many exciting contemplations. The basic elements of the process are described in Figure 9.1.

In principle, a search conference starts with the identification of a problem area, and it ends with the generation of concrete projects to meet the challenges that the conference has brought to light. Activities in a search conference are, as mentioned, divided between presentations and discussions in plenary, and work in groups, and the group work is usually conveyed to all participants in plenary. We will go through the process step-by-step.

The search conference is led by a staff of professionals (at least two people). In addition, it is often natural to involve local key players. The local participants can contribute local knowledge which is necessary to select the right stakeholders, but they can also function as a doorway to the local community.

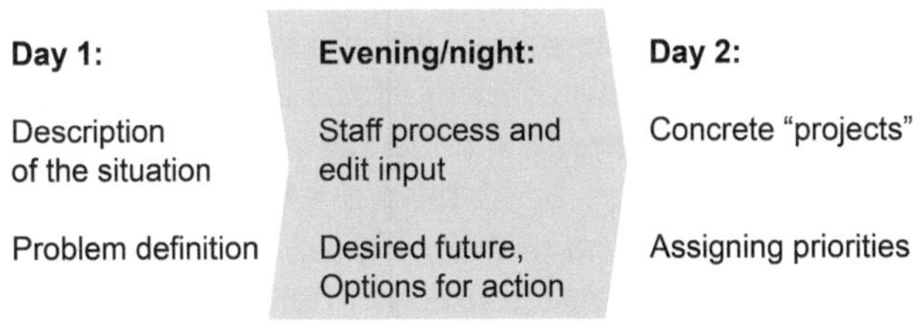

Day 1:	Evening/night:	Day 2:
Description of the situation	Staff process and edit input	Concrete "projects"
Problem definition	Desired future, Options for action	Assigning priorities

Figure 9.1   Phases of the search conference

Selecting Participants

The first challenge for staff organizing a search conference is selecting participants. A basic feature of the selection process is to find people who reflect as many aspects or interests of the issue in question as possible. It is important to make every effort to give all relevant stakeholders a voice in the conference. For example, in a conference that relates to a local community, participants should include children, youth, politicians, business managers, active women's groups and representatives of public administration. Thorough work must be done in selecting participants based on an assessment of who is important related to the specific issue at stake, and the potential participants must be judged to have the ability to cooperate in learning and planning processes. It is also important that the staff responsible for the conference establish as good an understanding as possible of the organization or community that is the focal point of the conference. One possible way of doing this is to interview all potential participants in advance, which will give the staff an understanding of who they are, provide an opportunity to convey what the search conference involves and motivate people to take part.

Staging

In the first phase of the actual search conference, the staff will introduce the direction or focus of the activity. It is up to the organizers of the conference to decide whether to keep a tight direction of the topic, or to have a more open process. For example, in cooperation with the Canadian Aviation Authority in Alberta, a search conference was held in which the topic was "increased efficiency and safety in regional aviation".

Such a precise definition of the topic implies tight direction. In a community context, it may be equally appropriate just to announce a general theme concerning a desirable future for the inhabitants. The topic of a search conference must, of course, be clarified with the initiating groups. A common way of starting the search is to let a local respected authority of the area (for example a mayor, an important professional or a local hero) frame the conference. This will be the first introduction, where everyone is together in plenary setting listening to the presentation.

How is the "Problem" Perceived?

At this stage, conference participants are divided in homogeneous groups with an assignment to describe how they understand and experience the issues at stake. Historical development should also be a part of this description, because it helps to locate the current situation in an historical perspective. An important perspective in this group work is that no experiences are wrong or right because the aim is to portray the broad understanding that is held by the participants. Therefore it is important to encourage participants to create an understanding that includes the breadth of the opinions that are conveyed through the group's work. If the conference is run in a manufacturing company, for example, it may be natural to form groups consisting of operators on the floor, mid-level operations management, marketing and sales,and top management. These groups should be as homogenous as possible. The groups' work is presented in a plenary session in such a way that the span of opinions is presented to everyone. It is important in this phase that the staff do not open up a discussion of what is right and wrong, but only give participants the opportunity to ask clarifying questions. All the groups present their work, for example by conveying the main points on flip charts. All the flip chart presentations are put up on the wall in the plenary hall and stay there throughout the entire conference. This allows participants to refer back to a broad understanding of how the problem was perceived.

Problem Definition and Desirable Future

The next step is an assignment where group members are asked to work on how they see the challenges for the future. Work is carried out in the same homogeneous groups as in the previous phase. Again, group members should be encouraged to actively support each other in order to provide a basis for broad problem clarification. This objective of this process is to identify what can be seen as the problem situation or definition of the problem. Visions of desirable futures can be woven into this phase, but some process leaders prefer to separate problem definition and visions of desirable future as two different phases in the course of the search conference. In both cases, the results of the teamwork are presented in plenary. Also at this stage it is important not to open up discussions of what is the right or wrong understanding of what characterizes the problem. The first day of the conference ends with reporting back from this problem-defining assignment. In the evening, participants will often have dinner together, and there is opportunity for discussion throughout the evening.

Staff's Organization of the Day's Work

During the evening, the staff prepare the next day's work. The staff's challenge is to organize the input from the first day's work, so that consistent categories are developed. Attention is directed at placing the visions of desirable futures in consistent categories that should be meaningful to the participants. If it turns out that problem definitions merge into visions of what a desirable future is (which may often be the case), it will be natural to integrate them under desirable futures.

A significant professional challenge for the staff is to understand what meaning participants attach to their utterances in order to create categories of the contributions from the groups in a way that makes them recognizable to the participants. An absolute requirement is that one keeps all text (as it is written on the flip charts) in its original form. This organization process is demanding and challenging work, which often leads to little sleep for the staff. The second day of the conference starts by sharing the staff's organization of the previous day. Special attention is devoted to understanding the different perspectives on what constitutes the problem in focus.

Assigning Priorities for Central Challenges

The second day starts with the staff asking participants whether they have thought about other factors related to the issues at stake, or if they have anything else that they would like to contribute. This could be either new perspectives or a further reflection on earlier presentations. Then the staff explains their reasons for the organization and test out if the structuring categories are in line with the participants' way of making sense of the situation. It is not necessarily a requirement that all agree on the way the actual categories structure the problems at hand. Opinions are now sorted by prioritizing what is important. If there are elements that participants do not recognize or disagree with, these will simply be that none of the participants would vote in favour of such an issue. The assigning of priorities can be carried out in different ways. An important challenge for the staff is to understand how disputed some topics can be. If it is likely that a discussion cannot be carried out in a plenary session, it is important to stop the discussion and let it continue in groups. This is an assessment that the staff have to make. If this is the case, it may be relevant to use groups which represent a cross-section of participants. Regardless, the result of this process is a list of problems in order of priority. This phase of the conference takes place within a plenary session in which visions of desirable future are presented in different categories of prioritized tasks. This list forms the basis for the next step, which is to develop alternatives for action.

Developing Alternatives for Action

There are several ways to approach this phase. To summarize, the purpose is to bring the visions of desirable futures as a goal for concrete problem-solving activity. At this point participants will be in a plenary setting, where the prioritized visions or problems which have now become development projects, are conveyed by posters or flip charts which are taped up on the walls of the room. Perhaps the most efficient way of staffing the various development projects is to let participants "vote with their feet". This means that participants sign in on the poster that presents the topic in which they are most interested. Thus, groups are formed which can immediately start working on concrete alternatives for action. Each group will make a plan for implementation. This should include a project plan which identifies who will take part, how the project will develop over time (a milestone plan) and an initial consideration of whether it will be important to recruit members other than those who have accepted the challenge at this point. An absolute requirement is that each group has identified who will participate in the first meeting and who would be responsible for calling and leading this meeting. A plenary session with a joint presentation concludes the search conference. Right at the end, the participants have to decide when the first follow-up meeting will take place.

Follow-up Meetings

After the search conference, there will be several groups working to solve the problems that were identified. This is a situation where there are a number of project groups at work. The follow-up meetings have several purposes. First, it is important to coordinate the activities of the various groups, so that people can build on and support each other's activities. Second, different groups will have encountered different obstacles and seen alternative possibilities, and this is of course information which might be important and useful for all groups. Third, the follow-up meetings create a structure which commits participants to report and subsequently coordinate activity. The number and frequency of follow-up meetings depends entirely on the particular development process.

The staff can conclude their tasks by writing a report of the search conference itself. In most cases, it is natural for the staff to continue as long as there are follow-up meetings, but after the conference, it is important to create local leadership for the development activities. An ideal development is that the professionals from the staff gradually withdraw.

10 The World Café – Active Involvement Through Meaningful Conversation

Mara Senese

How can we bring more energy into large groups?
How can we activate more people in a discussion?
How can we establish ownership for a project
when the project group is very large?

Introduction

Most meetings involving more than just a few people have a tendency to pacify most of the participants. The World Café is a simple work form which has interesting effects when it comes to activating the energy in larger groups. It brings people from different parts of an organization together in a new way, and teaches people new skills in communication through the way it is arranged.

The World Café is based on the assumption that a small group of people usually have lively and interesting conversations when they are sitting together in a café.

Just think about the phrase: The World Café. What images do you get? What do you associate with a phrase like that? I think about a café in Paris, with small intimate tables, and a relaxed atmosphere. Lively ideas are flying about. Everyone is participating actively. The enthusiasm rises as new ideas and insight pops up. The creativity is bubbling, and heads are bent over paper napkins filling up with new possibilities. The World Café has a positive connotation. We have nothing against being invited to a café together with friends. Meeting friends in a café is usual; it is something people often do to get inspiration. Cafés and creativity belong together.

Now think about our usual meetings at work. What images do you get when you think about these? Is it images of energetic, creative meeting points? Do you see a friendly exchange of ideas and thoughts? My image is of people sitting around large tables with a long distance between them. Someone sitting in front at the end of the table is presenting something. PowerPoint is used a lot. People are leaning backwards. Some are active, asking questions and proposing criticism. Most are passive, nodding affirmative now and then. The larger the group, the less the participation.

New ideas often arise when people are sitting in small groups and talking everyday talk. This happens all the time in organizations, but not in organized form. The problem is, that if there are traces of solutions in these conversations, they usually don't go very far. They are like seeds dying, without being properly sown. Often there are no mechanisms for seizing the energy created in these conversations, or moving it to a phase of solution.

Conversations happen all the time. How can we focus on them, and use them constructively? How can we build on the energy which arises around these conversations? One way is to use the World Café. The method trusts that individuals in a group can find common threads to weave with, and end up with a beautiful piece of clothing. The physical set-up of the World Café is based on the café idea as we know it. We have small tables spread across a large room. Around each table there are about 4–5 chairs.

To support the development of ideas, each table has a paper tablecloth, or a large flipchart sheet, and a set of coloured markers. Coffee cups and snacks are welcome at the table; other than these, the table should be cleared of books and papers.

An atmosphere of relaxed anticipation is created. In the background there might be music at low volume. The participants are welcomed at their arrival, and invited to a table. One creates a mix between people. Around each table there are people from different levels, departments and professions, and they are gathered to unite their thoughts regarding a specific topic.

It should be made clear that the group session will not end with a presentation in plenum. This will, among other things, make the groups more comfortable with opposing thoughts and opinions, and let these live side by side. We are not looking for agreement, but rather a more mutual understanding, and having the participants see the ideas and resources of the group. In the same way as a usual café, different viewpoints will contribute to inspired discussions and creativity.

It is important that there is a common theme for a world café, but this theme may hold great variation. The theme should be introduced as a question. The same question is the starting point for everyone, no matter how many tables and groups there are in the room. It is substantial that the theme is important to people, and that the question stimulates their imagination and creativity. An important criterion for success is to find a good formulation of themes and questions, questions that suit the audience, and are questions that matter.

Everyone should use the paper tablecloths actively while they are speaking. Ideas, questions, diagrams, symbols, drawings – everything that can contribute to catch the insight which is created along the way – should be scribbled down. The facilitator will help the groups get started on drawing and writing.

When people write a word down or draw something while they talk, the long monologues seem to disappear. The writings and drawings become a common reference, a kind of map of the discussion. It is easy to see where you have been, and where you want to go. And the map is visible for everyone, like a half structured collective memory for the group.

World Café in Practice

Not long ago I arranged a World Café for a township outside Oslo. The owner of the process was the head of the Cultural Department in this township. In the process of writing a plan for the cultural activities of the future, he realized that it would be important to bring in the various volunteers and clubs who were engaged in cultural activities in the area. Each group got some money from the township to do their activity. The money was shrinking in relationship to the increasing needs of the users. Everyone wanted more money for their activity.

The leader decided it was important to have a town meeting to discuss the needs and to help the users get a more holistic view of the situation. He was given a tip by a younger member of his department that the World Café might be a way to involve everyone and get the input they needed.

The leader was very nervous! This was so new for him. How would it be to get everyone involved? Would it all turn into chaos? There were only three hours available and the amount of input needed was so great that it was hard to imagine that anything constructive could come of it.

He was worried about how the people would react since they were used to being passive at town meetings, just expecting to listen to those who had the most to say. Would they resist being asked to participate fully and say what they were thinking in diverse groups?

Most of them didn't know each other outside their own area. In fact there were rival groups that had vied for money for years. Would they come into conflict with each other, getting stuck in old patterns?

The leader didn't say much at the planning meetings. I noticed that he mostly just bit his lower lip and kept quiet. The younger team member told me of the leader's anxiety.

This didn't make me feel any more confident. I even began to wonder if the World Café would work for them?

The big night came. People arrived and became wide-eyed at the unusual table arrangement. They commented on the music. Most of them stood around the edges waiting until someone they knew showed up. Little by little they were shown to their seats. The groups were arranged in advance to ensure diversity but it turned out that we had to change them around anyway because some people didn't show up and we found out that we wanted to include the members of the Cultural Department. We did this by just asking people to move around until they were with people who worked in different areas. It was a little chaotic but people quickly found their place. They were accommodating and curious.

After the concept of World Café was presented, the first set of questions was given to the whole group. They had 20 minutes to share their ideas and write down their comments, insights and questions on the tablecloth. They were encouraged to draw and soon the whole thing got going. High energy began to fill the room. Laughter bubbled up, heads bowed over the drawings and the diagrams. They shared their world, their problems, and their solutions. The room filled with enthusiasm and activity.

After 20 minutes were up, the groups were asked to choose a host who would stay at the table while the others were to leave and go "out into the world". Moving each to a different table, a whole new configuration of groups was established. The ideas, drawings and questions that were made by the original group, were explained by the host to the new group. Then each new group member shared what had happened at their table. Once again, the energy began to grow, the discussions got deeper. Similarities and differences began to appear. New ideas and associations were added to the tablecloth. Laughter filled the room and it became alive with possibilities.

The bell sounded and everyone had to go "home", bringing with them the experience of their "travels". It is always fun to tell other people about your new experiences, so it was easy to relate the ideas and suggestions as well as the conflicting desires that were encountered at the other tables. Now they were to incorporate any new thoughts that expanded their own original ideas. Any new insights or solutions were written down and elaborated on.

When it was time for a break, many groups kept talking, finding it hard to pull away from their engaging conversations. Several more rounds of questions, travel and back home again, concluded the session. As a final summing up, we asked each table to report how they experienced the evening. The response was overwhelming. They were enthusiastic about how challenging and fun it was to contribute ideas and solutions to common problems. Surprise over discovering the commonality of challenges led to a sympathetic understanding of each other. Ideas that could work for many sectors at the same time bubbled forth. They found ways in which to support and use each other in a positive way. They were grateful for the opportunity and thanked the leader for initiating such a fun and unusual approach.

The leader beamed his satisfaction and took their suggestions to heart. He was willing to change a process that had already been established to incorporate the new ideas. His willingness and openness to the ideas seemed to come from the understanding he had obtained by listening to so many different people at his table.

The leader's courage to take a risk was essential to get something new to happen in the community. Courage to go against the stream is needed in today's world of challenges. It isn't always easy to try something revolutionary in the face of the prestige that often accompanies such a position.

We ended the evening on a high note of expectation and willingness to work toward new solutions. Of course this is only the beginning of such work, but the enthusiasm that replaced typical negativity and scepticism at such town meetings gave a lot of energy to the team that would continue to work on this project. They felt like they were now part of a larger team that would help them and back them with renewed energy.

The volunteers also seemed to be activated to try new solutions and returned home enriched with new contacts. There was a sense of wholeness in the group. The identity of the individuals had expanded to embrace the entire township and not just their own little sector and own little organization.

We begin to see that it is not the piece of paper that may come out of such a meeting that is the important thing. It is the energy and commitment that are activated through the process that will be most essential in changing the way an organization behaves. The emphasis is on process. This needs to be followed up but will be easier to do because of the initial positive energy generated at this first meeting.

So we have taken informal conversation and turned it into a source of strategic creative direction-finding for an organization.

Concluding Comment

Creating a community is one of the most constructive approaches to support change in a culture characterized by individualism. These processes do not happen by themselves. The World Café is just one of many structured fora that have the ability to bring people from different positions together for constructive and creative work. New ways to facilitate the bringing together of people across traditional divisions will contribute to effects of this type.

11 Resolving Workplace Conflict Using Interest-based Processes

Ann W. Martin

Organizational growth and even survival are facilitated by joint problem-solving rather than competition, which is why it is worthwhile to find a problem-solving method that builds constructively on differences. Interest bargaining is the term for a problem-solving process that focuses on the underlying needs or interests of the parties or individuals involved. It is useful when different perspectives block solution. The process, outlined below, invites participants – either two individuals or more – to move past the particular *positions* they hold and converse about the needs or interests, the worries and concerns, that lead them to take those positions. Often it is discovered that while the positions appeared to be in opposition, the underlying interests might be met by an altogether different solution than has been proposed (Fisher and Ury 1981).

Conflict is a fact of organizational life. Differences in status or role among individuals, differences in goals or focus among departments or functions and the struggle over limited resources all generate conflict within an organization. This is true within all organizations but even more so in team-based organizations where decision-making is expected to be collaborative and authority is shared. The more open, collaborative organization creates an opportunity for better ideas and greater commitment to ideas. It also means more different perspectives have to be taken into account when plans and decisions are made, and a natural consequence of engaging different perspectives is disagreement.

To complicate matters, differences in personality, values and style exist among the individuals in each organization and group. Often when a conflict within an organization comes to a head, the individuals will claim that, "It's a personality problem" or "We just can't get along". Individual differences do, certainly, contribute to conflict, but they are often exacerbated by context – those role, status, focus or resource constraints that are part of the fabric of organizational life. The interest-based approach to resolving conflict allows people to articulate their needs and understand better what organizational requirements may underlie a particular view.

Interest-based problem-solving is a means to address immediate problems and often builds better relationships so that similar kinds of problems can be avoided in the future. However, this process may not address deep conflicts where the issues are fundamentally intertwined with an individual's identity. Deep issues around gender or race or religion, particularly where there is a history of oppression, call for a different conflict resolution process (Rothman 1997). Interest-based strategies are most useful when what is sought are practical solutions in the workplace.

The Process

The most common approach to disagreement is to assume that the "right" answer is one's own while the other party assumes the same. These right answers are positions. A position is a single solution to a problem (Fisher and Ury 1981). Often in organizational life these are presented as unilateral propositions or proposals. Another assumption, often unrecognized, is that the universe of possible solutions is limited. Either your proposal or mine must succeed. Therefore, if your position prevails, you win and I lose. Conflict escalates as we try to convince each other of our position.

However, other assumptions are possible, and these are the assumptions underlying interest-based processes. One is the assumption that there may be a solution that yields something for both of us, one in which we can find mutual gain. Behind our original position are needs and concerns that can be characterized as "interests". The exploration of this possibility for mutual gain requires that we set aside our positions and return to our interests – and then seek ways to meet those interests. Second is the assumption that we can, by seeking to understand the other through clarifying questions and careful listening, see that ours is not the only possible solution.

This assumption that mutual gain is possible is itself based on the assumption that while two parties may have different interests, those interests are not necessarily in conflict. These are not to be confused with mutual interests, which the parties may have as well. Figure 11.1 illustrates the distinction:

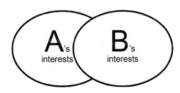

Figure 11.1   Participants' interests

In the centre, A's and B's interests overlap; those are mutual interests. These are often broad values, such as corporate success, valuable products, a respectful workplace. Beyond the centre on both sides are interests that are not the same. Parties can agree on their mutual interests in principle, but it is their differing interests that block agreement. For an interest-based discussion to work well, each party must act on an understanding that the different interests of the other, while not shared, *are legitimate*, at least for the other. They must be willing to hear the interests of the other and consider them of equal importance as to their own in finding a solution.

As Fisher and Ury originally laid out *interest*-based discussion in their book, *Getting to Yes* (1981), there are four guides for action in this process. These can be used whether there are two people in conflict trying to resolve an issue between them, two teams, or many people in dispute over the resolution to a problem.

1. *Separate the people from the problem.* To solve problems effectively, you should focus on the problem and set aside whatever opinions or fears you have about the other party. Figuratively speaking, instead of facing the other person in confrontation, you might sit side by side and together face the problem. This can actually be done by writing the problem on a flipchart and seating yourselves side by side facing the flipchart.

2. *Focus on interests, not positions.* To do this, first state the positions that exist. Mr L thinks the solution should be this, Mr S thinks it should be this. Then take turns listing the underlying needs and concerns that inform these positions. It's good to have them written on a board or flipchart in front of you. There is no need to label whose interest is whose; everyone will know anyway, and it may turn out that a number of the needs and concerns are the same. It is important to get to the real interests, which you do by asking "why" several times. For example, if one group is insisting that meetings be held before the shift ends, the stated interest may be "union rules". Then you would need to ask for more explanation, "why does this matter?" The responses will probably lead to mention of fair pay and even respect. These interests, fairness and respect, become measures of a solution. There may be a way, for example, to hold meetings after the shift ends if there is some compensation or even if there is simply an acknowledgement of respect for the workgroup's time and effort.

3. *Generate options for mutual gain.* In this step, whether there are two people or several, the task is to brainstorm ideas to meet as many of the listed interests as possible. The interests become the equivalent of criteria for a solution. Brainstorming is a specific kind of activity with its own ground rules, one of which is that participants must speak out whatever ideas come to mind in order to encourage many ideas. This means there must be no judgment of ideas as they are said and written down. Participants should continue brainstorming until they have several ideas; even unrealistic ideas count. Once the brainstorming session is over, the list of options is easily reduced if parties are asked for three or four ideas that meet their interests *and* at least

some of the other party's. Sometimes at this point a new solution becomes clear. Sometimes it takes more work. A question to ask is, "What can we do to this option to make it meet more of your interests?" This, in effect, allows for the parties to combine elements of various solutions.

4. *Look for objective standards to help decision making.* These standards can be a set of well-established rules or practices, the word of an expert, the opinion of a trusted third party or even an accepted fair procedure (such as one cuts the cake, and the other chooses first). What is most challenging here is to agree on what is "objective". If one party claims that what another company does should be a standard, that standard is only good if the other party agrees that it should be. Or if one party holds up the opinion of an expert, that opinion can only be useful in this situation if the other party agrees. Sometimes just the process of looking for a standard helps the parties narrow the range of their differences and get closer to agreement. Don't confuse "objective standards" with facts. Facts and the meaning attached to facts are often themselves in dispute. However, if parties in disagreement can agree that they need more information, they can make the search for that information a joint project. When information is sought jointly, the information found is more likely to be credible (and therefore useful) in the views of both parties.

Making the Process Work, a Workplace Case

A small company making specialized metal parts for the automobile industry has come under extreme pressure to operate more economically. At the urging of the owners, the operations manager of the company has decided that a shift to lean manufacturing practices is the only way to improve operations. She calls a meeting of the leadership team in the plant to explain and plan for this change. At this meeting she encounters significant resistance. The engineers say that shifting manufacturing practices is a waste of valuable time when there is so much pressure to produce; they ask why people shouldn't just work harder and faster. The three manufacturing team leaders say very little, but she hears later from the union leader that people believe they are already working to capacity and that neither new systems nor increased pressure could change anything. Furthermore, the leader says workers think the whole idea is to make them work harder and faster, just as the engineers said.

Here is how it might work if the operations manager were to take an interest-based approach inside her plant. She must reframe the issue as problem-solving, bringing the parties together to face the common problem of insufficiently economical production according to the demands of the customer. Steps she might take:

1. To begin with she would meet separately with the leaders of engineering and of manufacturing to understand the needs and concerns of each group. She would ask questions for clarification and listen carefully with respect. In effect, by doing this she is *separating the people from the problem.* She avoids stereotyping either group according to their roles in the company, and she invites them to surpass those roles and put their attention on the shared problem. In the case of manufacturing team leaders, her willingness to meet separately signals that she is as eager to hear from them as from the engineers. Let's suppose the interests come out in the way illustrated in Table 11.1:

Table 11.1   Participants' interests

Engineers	Manufacturing Teams	Operations Manager
Efficiency	Avoiding accidents associated with speedup and stress	Timeliness
Straightforward solutions	Clear instructions	Workable solutions
Respect for their capacity	Respect for their skills	Economy
A chance to participate in improvement planning	A chance to participate in improvement planning	

2. The next step is to bring the groups together to *focus on interests*, the needs and concerns of engineers, work teams and her own interests as operations manager. Instead of focusing on her position, which is to adopt lean manufacturing practices, she focuses on the need to improve operations and shares her interests (see Table 11.1) with the group. This expands the arena for problem-solving and redefines the question as follows: how can we improve operations while meeting the interests of engineering, manufacturing and the customer (as expressed by the operations manager)?

3. The third step, following the principles of interest-based problem-solving, is to *generate options together*. Who engages in this work is a practical decision: it could be the original leadership groups; it could include other critical players in plant; it should include union leaders and others who are needed as champions of change. This can begin as a simple brainstorming activity, seeking possible answers

to their redefined question. Ideas generated are then refined, either by small teams willing to work on clusters of ideas, or by the entire group if it is no larger than 15 people. Refined ideas are brought back to the larger group for quick approval. As the options are generated, areas for mutual planning of improvements should arise. One of the options might still be to adopt lean manufacturing practices, but this could be modified so that engineers and manufacturing workers are involved in researching and installing the most relevant of these practices. If the interest in timeliness is given attention, the planning decisions will have target dates.

4. As difficult choices are made, the group can seek *objective standards* to help. In this case, such standards might be the experience of similar plants with manufacturing changes, statistics on the impact and cost of adopting lean manufacturing practices, and even the expectations of the customers. What will make these standards objective, however, is their adoption by participants with different perspectives. If a small team, perhaps only a pair of people, from both manufacturing and engineering do the research together, the knowledge they bring back is likely to be acceptable to different views, and perceived as "objective".

The interest-based approach has been found workable when the issues were broad, as in this case, or, for example, in the assignment of overtime in a 1,000-person manufacturing plant. In that case, operations managers and union leaders came to the table to address the issue. Interest-based discussion has also been used successfully in environmental disputes, where community representatives and company leaders agreed on the requirements for a waste incinerator.

The approach can also be useful when the issue is as narrow as a dispute over work space between two colleagues. Once individuals can agree to listen to what is behind each others' positions (the interests) they may be open to more creative solutions.

How Do You Know the Process is Successful?

If interests have been articulated by the parties to a dispute, the simplest measure of success is the extent to which those interests have been met. A solution that is "workable" but does not meet the parties' interests will not in the end be a successful solution. In the manufacturing scenario above, the operations manager could simply have ordered the change. While that might have looked good on paper, it would risk resentment and non-compliance by the people who would have to carry out the changes. Such an order would also leave unexplored the power of a new working relationship between critical groups in the plant.

12 Learning Histories

Emil A. Røyrvik

All organizations have some sort of a collective knowledge base or knowledge repertoire that employees use, maintain and develop through daily work. This may be to adopt everything from written routines and work methods, software and manuals, to experience-based knowledge, intuition and informal habits and routines. In addition to the internal knowledge use and development, organizations adopt knowledge from external sources. This happens, for example, by recruiting new employees and by giving employees continuing education. This type of knowledge acquisition is often not intimately connected to the organization's value creating activities, and knowledge must therefore be made relevant or internalized in the organization before it is put to use. The knowledge transferred in such relationships intervenes directly in how organizations perform their tasks, and how they create value. Learning histories may help to contribute to a deeper understanding of learning processes in organizational practices, and the vital mechanisms enabling the work arena to become a fruitful learning arena.

What is a Learning History?

Learning histories as a method was developed at MIT and had as a point of departure the perspective that learning processes are difficult to document quantitatively. The method is used to document and improve the organization's ability to learn. The histories document change and facilitate individual and organizational reflection. One of the key persons developing the method, George Roth, defines them the following way: "Learning histories are a formalized approach for capturing and presenting learning processes in organizations" (Roth 1996: 5).

As a result or "product" the learning stories can be considered a type of externalized organizational memory. They are produced to provide answers to *how*, *why* and *when* learning takes place in practice in an organization (or a networked organization). Their power lies in their ability to show and convey many actors' perspectives of more or less controversial or important events in the organization's work life. In contrast to "argumentative texts", as, for example, conventional reports or evaluations that are aimed at giving a specific opinion or interpretation of something, learning histories are narrative texts that do not aim to present the one correct interpretation or meaning of events, but rather to open up more and alternative interpretations. As such they are an attempt to highlight some of the premises and constraints for change – and learning processes in organizations (Hatling 2001).

A learning history is in short a written history of important events in a company's or organization's life, about a new initiative, an important innovation, a major event, or the like. The stories vary in length, but must not be so long that they exhaust readers. One of the main motives to create learning histories is that they are going to be a catalyst for change-oriented discussions at many levels within the organization.

In relation to the stories a series of organized discussions about them are conducted among members of the organization. Both members who have been involved in the activities documented by the stories and other members are part of the discussions. The goal of these discussions is to create a shared space where different meanings and perspectives are brought to the table, and where a fertile ground for approaching more shared understandings of problems and solutions is created. They are also important because change often requires concerted actions across organizational boundaries within the company.

There are four main reasons for the usefulness of learning stories:

1. Learning histories create trust in the organization because different views and perspectives on an issue or event are voiced. This is true both in the story itself, and in the subsequent discussions.

2. Learning histories are particularly effective in addressing difficult issues, and learning histories can give voice to issues that are surrounded by taboo and an air of "taken-for-granted" or "non-discussable". The document's structure, which is an exchange between direct quotes from organizational members and the authors' comments, creates a template for more open, critical and creative discussions later.

3. Learning histories have proven to be effective to disseminate knowledge across organizational boundaries. The distinctive shape of the "discussion-like" history makes it easier for readers to recognize themselves and relate other's learning experiences to their own reality.

4. Learning histories are well-suited for establishing general knowledge about management and leadership. They are specifically designed to enable learning from a particular event, but it is also possible to draw knowledge from it on a more general management level.

A learning history is a document that is disseminated purposefully to help an organization to become more aware of its own efforts to learn. The story utilizes the extensive use of the participants' own stories, as well as external evaluations of the story (Roth and Kleiner 1995). The story wanders back and forth between different perspectives on events that have taken place. The different perspectives each represent a separate, limited and legitimate piece of a larger picture. The aim of presenting them together is that the organization can then learn more about what has happened, why it happened, and what one should do in the future.

"Technical" Production and Reading guide

The technique used in writing learning stories is to use a two-column format in the presentations. In the column on the right side are only direct quotes from participants in the stories, while the left column allows for comments and questions to the direct quotes. The left side column is reserved for the producers of the stories, the "outsiders", and their voice will both provide enlightening comments about the context of the direct quotations, and act as a form of indirect questions and comments that opens up the significance and meaning of the quotes presented in the right column. Specifically, the text should not be read column by column, but rather the "normal" way from left to right. First the paragraph in the left column is read, followed by its adjacent paragraph in the right hand column, then the next paragraph in the left column, and so on. In this way there is a form of dialogue, not only between the different "insider" voices in the right column, but also between the "outsider" voice in the left column and the insider voices in the right column.

Key Characteristics of Learning Histories

A learning history evolves around so-called *noticeable results*. These are events that members of an organization consider significant, and include both "hard" business results and "soft" human effects. These results are defined on the basis of an internal business process, which also means that there will be differing views on them. To arrive upon noticeable results is one of the most important activities in the production of learning histories.

A learning history is meant for a wider audience than those who contribute with experiences to the stories. It describes the experiences of a few, but is intended as an input in discussions for an entire organization. The data is generated through reflective conversations. Data collection takes place in contexts where people can reflect on what they have achieved, as well as over frustrations and attitudes. Interview guides are not used. Data collection has more the character of a conversation about some topics. The learning history is written as a "jointly-told tale". This is a technique adopted from ethnography and cultural anthropology, where participants (informants) and researchers tell stories on equal terms "side by side". When it comes to layout, it is set up in the two-column format illustrated in Figure 12.1.

A team of insiders and outsiders create the history. The team consists of people who work in the organization and external researchers. The document couples interpretations and conjectures with observable data. Readers must always be able to connect assessments, interpretations and statements to the data they have at hand. This is methodologically important, so that the stories are not reduced to just "organizational gossip". The aim is to find means to enable and improve the organizational dialogue. Learning histories should not be assessed on the basis of the text(s) alone. In the process,

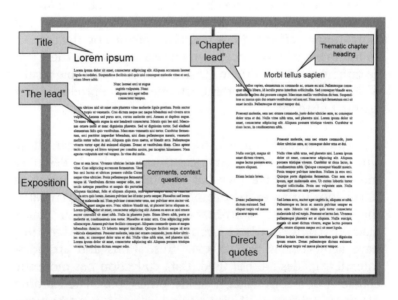

Figure 12.1   Structure of a learning history

there are three main possibilities for reflective dialogue: during the interviews; in different phases of the distillation of the story-process; and in the dissemination process. In the learning histories approach we distinguish between assessment, measurement and evaluation. This is done to liberate organizational members from the increasing plague of predetermined measurement and evaluation regimes.

Why Write Learning Stories?

Learning histories is a technique to document learning and facilitate learning processes in organizations. However, all initiatives and measures designed to create more learning organizations are suffering from the difficulty in quantifying learning. Better learning organizations do not necessarily lead to results in the short term, for example in the form of better earnings, but can contribute to making organizations more adaptable, agile and resilient to changing environmental and societal conditions, enhance their innovation capabilities and in other ways make them more efficient and competitive. However, without some form of evaluation of the measures taken it is difficult to learn *organizationally* from the experiences accumulating, in order to get a better grasp of what works and what does not.

Learning histories is thus a way to collect and disseminate experiences and understandings between *groups* of people and not just from a few individuals, such as managers. They do not provide a complete picture of why something is a success or a failure, but may help to reveal underlying relationships and causes that are not straightforward to assess in light of the results achieved. They may contribute to bring more subtle and weak action and reaction-patterns into the light because they focus on a relatively detailed level of description of events as seen from different people's diverse perspectives. With its rich descriptions, learning histories contribute to revealing complex causalities and the various factors (such as environment, culture, networks) that are crucial for organizational learning.

Progress in Learning History Projects

First determine a planning stage, the definition and scope of the document, and decide which audience(s) are to learn from the experiences documented. The noticeable results you would want to start out with are defined in the planning stage.

Then conduct a series of retrospective and reflective conversation-based interviews with selected individuals from the organization to bring out different perspectives. The selection of interviewees must be broad.

Subsequently, refine and distil the material, together with other written and oral documentation, into a coherent set of themes that the stories can be built around. These themes can fruitfully instantiate and revolve around paradoxes or dilemmas (Røyrvik and Wullf 2004).

The story is written in form and genre that fits the theme and story best (based on a set of predefined structures of narrative forms), and in the specified two-column format. There are several examples of successful use of web-based multi-media learning histories (Røyrvik and Bygdås 2004).

The story must then pass through a validation and adjustment phase, a collaborative effort between the ones who are the primary authors of the story, and those who are interviewed and are participants in the story.

Finally, the learning history is disseminated in different ways and through various channels, such as presented on a corporate web-site, handed out on paper and presented at workshops, being read and discussed at introductory courses for new employees and the like. The key here is to establish spaces for dialogue around the story in the organization.

Summary

Learning histories may be regarded as a kind of organizational memory. The production of learning histories is done to illustrate how, why and when learning takes place in practice in organizations. The main power of the story projects is their ability to display many actors' different perspectives on significant events, among other things to convey the breadth of member's assessments of the events, and thus to form a basis for more real discussions about important issues within the organization.

References

Argyris, C. 1986. Skilled incompetence. *Harvard Business Review* 64(5), 74–79.

Argyris, C., Putnam, R., and Smith, D.M. 1985. *Action Science: Concepts, Methods and Skills for Research and Intervention.* San Francisco, CA: Jossey-Bass.

Argyris, C. and Schön, D.A. 1978. *Organizational Learning: A Theory of Action Perspective.* New York: Addision-Wesley.

Argyris, C. and Schön, D.A. 1996. *Organizational Learning II Theory, Method, and Practice.* New York: Addison Wesley.

Bass, B.M. 1990. From transactional to transformational leadership: Learning to share the vision. *Organizational Dynamics* (Winter): 19–31.

Blanchard, K.F. and Johnson, S. 1983. *The One Minute Manager.* London: Willow.

Bolman, L.G. and Deal, T.E. 1984. *Modern Approaches to Understanding and Managing Organizations.* San Francisco: Jossey-Bass Publishers.

Borum, F. 1980. A Power Strategy Alternative to Organization Development. *Organization Studies* 1/2, 123–46.

Bradley, H., Erickson, M., Stephenson, C., et al. 2000. *Myths at Work*. Cambridge: Polity Press.

Bråten, S. 1973. Model monopoly and communication: Systems theoretical notes on democratization. *Acta Sociologica* 16(2), 98–107.

Charmaz, K. 2006. *Constructing Grounded Theory. A Practical Guide Through Qualitative Analysis*. London: Sage.

Collins, J. 2001. *From Good to Great*. New York: HarperCollins.

Corbin, J. and Strauss, A. 2008. *Basics of Qualitative Research* 3rd edn. Newbury Park: Sage.

Crozier, M. 1964. *The Bureaucratic Phenomenon*. Chicago: University of Chicago Press.

deGeus A. 1997. *The Living Company: Habits for Survival in a Turbulent Business Environment*. Boston, MA: Harvard Business School Press.

Davenport, T. 1995. The Fad that Forgot People, *Fast Company*, inaugural issue.

Dewey, J. 1966. *Democracy and Education: An Introduction to the Philosophy of Education*. Carbondale: Southern Illinois University Press (originally published 1916).

Dewey, J. 1991. *Logic: The Theory of Inquiry*. Carbondale: Southern Illinois University Press (originally published 1938).

Dewey, J. 1991. *The Public and its Problems*. Ohio: University Press (originally published 1927).

Edvinsson, L. and Malone, M.S. 1997. *Intellectual Capital: Realizing your Company's True Value by Finding Its Hidden Roots*. New York: Harper Business.

Elden, M. and Levin, M. 1991. Co-generative learning. Bringing Participation into Action. In Whyte, W.F. (ed.) *Participatory Action Research*. Newbury Hill: Sage.

Emery, F. 1959. *Characteristics of Socio-Technical Systems*. London, Tavistock Institute of Human Relations, Doc. 527.

Emery, F., ed. 1969. *Systems Thinking*. Harmondsworth: Penguin.

Emery, F., ed. 1981. *Systems Thinking, Volume Two*. Harmondsworth: Penguin.

Emery, F. and Oeser, O.A. 1958. *Information, Decision and Action*. Melbourne: Melbourne University Press.

Emery, F. and Thorsrud, E.E. 1969. *Form and Content in Industrial Democracy*. London: Tavistock.

Emery, F.E. and Trist, E.L. 1965. The causal texture of organizational environments. *Human Relations* 18, 21–32.

Emery, M. 1999. *Searching. The Power of Community Search Conferences*. Amsterdam: John Benjamins.

Engelstad, P.H. and Haugen, R. 1979. *Søkekonferansen Skjervøy, i går, i dag og i morgen (Search Conferences, the Past, the Present and the Future)*. Oslo: API.

Fisher, R. and Ury, W. 1981. *Getting to YES*. Harmondsworth: Penguin Books.

French, W.L., Bell, C.H. and Zwaki, R.A. 1994. *Organization Development and Transformation*. Boston: Irwin.

Glaser, B. and Strauss, A. 1967. *The Discovery of Grounded Theory*. Chicago: Aldine.

Greenberg, E. 1975. The consequences of worker participation and control: A clarification of the theoretical literature. *Social Science Quarterly* (Sept): 225–42.

Greenwood, D.J. and Levin, M. 1998. *Introduction to Action Research Social Research for Social Change*. Thousand Oaks: Sage.

Greenwood, D.J. and Levin, M. 2007. *Introduction to Action Research Social Research for Social Change* 2nd edn. Thousand Oaks: Sage.

Gustavsen, B. and Engelstad, P.H. 1986. The design of conferences and the evolving role of democratic dialogue in changing working life. *Human Relations* 39(2), 101–16.

Hammer, M. 1990. Re-engineering work: Don't automate, obliterate. *Harvard Business Review*. July–August pp. 104–112.

Hammer, M. and Champy, J. 1993. *Reengineering the Corporation a Manifesto of Business Revolution.* London: Nicholas Brealey Publishing.

Hatch, M.J. and Cunliffe, A.L. 2006. *Organization Theory, Modern, Symbolic, and Postmodern Perspectives.* Oxford: Oxford University Press.

Hatling, M., ed. 2001. *Fortellingens fortrylling. Bruk av fortellinger i bedrifters kunnskapsarbeid. (Use of Storytelling in Company Knowledge Work).* Oslo: Fortuna Forlag.

Herbst, P. 1977. *Alternativ til hierarkisk organisasjon. (Alternatives to Hierarchies)* Oslo: Tanum – Norli.

Kaplan, R.S. and Norton, D.P. 1996. *The Balanced Scorecard Translating Strategy into Action.* Boston: Harvard Business School Press.

Kotter, J.P. 1996. *Leading Change.* Boston: Harvard Business School Press.

Levin, M. 1984. Worker Participation in the Design of New Technology. In *Design of Work in Automated Manufacturing Systems,* ed. T. Martin. Oxford: Pergamon Press, 97–103.

Levin, M. 1998. Technology transfer is organizational development. An investigation in the relationship between technology transfer and organizational change. *International Journal of Technology Management* 14(2/3/4), 297–308.

Lewin, K. 1943. Forces behind food habits and methods of change. *Bulletin of the National Research Council* 108, 35–65.

Lewin, K. 1952. *Field Theory in Social Science: Selected Theoretical Papers by Kurt Lewin*. London: Tavistock.

March, J. 1991. Exploration and exploitation in organizational learning. *Organization Science* 2(1), 71–87.

March, J. and Simon, H. 1958. *Organizations*. Chichester: John Wiley & Sons.

Maslow, A. 1954. *Motivation and Personality*. New York: Harper.

Mayo, E. 1933. *The Human Problems of an Industrial Civilization*. New York: MacMillan.

Micklethwait, J. and Wooldridge, A. 1996. *The Witch Doctors*. London: Times Business Press.

Mintzberg, H. 2004. *Managers Not MBAs*. Berret-Koehler Publishers Inc., San Fransisco CA

Morgan, G. 1986. *Images of Organization*. Newbury Park: Sage.

Morgan, G. 1988. *Riding the Waves of Change. Developing Managerial Competencies for a Turbulent World*. London: Jossey Bass.

Nelson, R.R. and Winter, S.S. 1982. *An Evolutionary Theory of Economic Change*. Cambridge: The Bekamp Press of Harvard University.

Nonaka, I. and Takeuchi, H. 1995. *The Knowledge Crating Company How Japanese Companies Create the Dynamics of Innovation*. Oxford: Oxford University Press.

Northouse, P. 2004. *Leadership. Theory and Practice*. Thousand Oaks: Sage Publications.

Pateman, C. 1970. *Participation and Democratic Theory*. Cambridge: Cambridge University Press.

Peters, T. and Waterman, R. 1982. *In Search of Excellence*. New York: Warner Books.

Pfeffer, J. and Sutton, R.I. 1999. *The Knowing-Doing Gap*. Boston: HBS Press.

Pfeffer, J. and Sutton, R.I. 2006. *Hard Facts, Dangerous Half-Truths & Total Nonsense*. Boston: HBS Press.

Polanyi, M. 1966. *The Tacit Dimension*. New York: Doubleday.

Reason, P. and Bradbury, H. 2007. *Handbook of Action Research* 2nd edn. Thousand Oaks: Sage.

Rogers, C. 1969. *Freedom to Learn: A View of What Education Might Become* 1st edn. Columbus, OH: Charles Merill.

Roth, G. and Kleiner, A. 1995. *Learning About Organizational Learning – Creating a Learning History*. Cambridge, MA: MIT Center for Organizational Learning Working Paper, April.

Roth, G. 1996. *Learning Histories: Using Documentation to Assess and Facilitate Organizational Learning*. MIT Center for Organizational Learning Working Paper, Cambridge, MA.

Rothman, J., 1997. *Resolving Identity-based Conflict in Nations, Organizations and Communities*. New York: Jossey Bass.

Røyrvik, E.A. and Bygdås, A.L. 2004. Knowledge Hyperstories. The Use of ICT Enhanced Storytelling in Organizations. In *Living Knowledge: The Dynamics of Professional Service Work*, eds A. Carlsen, et al. Basingstoke: Palgrave Macmillan, 184–203.

Røyrvik, E.A. and Wulff, E. 2004. Dancing the Dilemmas: The Mythological Enabling of Collective Action. In *Living Knowledge: The Dynamics of Professional Service Work*, eds A. Carlsen, et al. Basingstoke: Palgrave Macmillan, 115–139.

Ryle, G. 1949. *The Concept of Mind*. Chicago: University of Chicago Press.

Schön, D.A. 1983. *The Reflective Practitioner How Professionals Think in Action*. New York: Basic Books.

Senge, P. 1990. *The Fifth Discipline the Art and Practice of the Learning Organization*. New York: Doubleday.

Skjervheim, H. 1974. Objectivism and the Study of Man (Part I). *Inquiry* 17(1–4), 213–39.

Taylor, F.W. 1911. *The Principles of Scientific Management*. New York: W.W. Norton & Company.

Tempte, T. 1991. The Chair of Tutankhamun Art and Knowledge. In *Dialogue and Technology*, ed. Görantzon, B. and M. Florin. Berlin: Springer Verlag.

Thorsrud, E. and Emery, F. 1970. *Mot en ny bedriftsorganisasjon*. Oslo: Tanum – Norli.

Trist, E. 1981. *The Evolution of Socio-technical Systems a Conceptual Framework and an Action Research Program*. Toronto: Ontario Quality of Working Life Centre.

Trist, E. and Bamfort, K. 1951. Some social and psychological consequences of the longwall method of coal getting. *Human Relations* 4, 3–38.

Weber, M. 1978. *Economy and Society*. Los Angeles: University of California Press (originally published 1922).

Weick, K.E. 1995. *Sensemaking in Organizations*. Thousand Oaks: Sage.

Welch, J. and Byrne, J. 2001. *Jack: Straight from the Gut*. New York: Warner Business Books.

Wittgenstein, L. 1953. *Philosophical Investigations* (G.E.M. Anscombe, trans.). Oxford: Basil Blackwell.

Womack, J.P., Jones, D.T. and Roos, D. 1990. *The Machine that Changed the World*. New York. Rawson Associates.

Index

Note: page numbers in *italic type* refer to Figures; those in **bold type** refer to Tables.